Front Cover Art: Devil Homura by Deviantart user Mary-Ko
http://mary-ko.deviantart.com/

Commentary: © Brian McAfee, 2016

Puella Magi Madoka Magica, all related spinoffs, their associated characters, concepts, designs, indicia, and story are copyright Magica Quartet/SHAFT/Aniplex and their original creators and are used under the doctrine of fair use for commentary, critique and academic/educational purposes.

The opinions presented here are those of the individuals providing them and do not necessarily reflect those of Magica Quartet, SHAFT, Aniplex, their partners or licensees.

Special thanks to Carrie Keranen, Cassandra Morris, Cristina Vee, and Sarah Williams, who all contributed their thoughts, encouraged, and inspired me while writing this book.

Special thanks also to my daughter Samantha, who encouraged me through the entire writing process and contributed several ideas which made their way into these pages.

And thanks also to Suzanne Yee, who took my clumsy words and made them into a book.

www.madokarevelations.com

REVELATIONS

An In-Depth Look at the Themes and Symbols of

PUELLA MAGI MADOKA MAGICA

By
Brian J. McAfee

Edited by Suzanne Yee

Createspace Independent Publishing, USA

Table of Contents

Preface..v

Introduction...viii

The Case for Faust...1

The Christian Perspective...9

The Undiscovered Country..17

The Mermaid and the Nutcracker..28

The Schism, or How *Rebellion* Split the Fandom...............43

Symbology...53

Deciphering the Runes..70

There's No Way I'll Ever Regret It.......................................76

Color Coded for Your Convenience....................................84

Deconstructing the Magical Girl..89

Moments: The Theme of Balance......................................95

Epilogue..104

References..110

Preface

> I know how to make the people happy:
> But I've never been so embarrassed: not
> That they've been used to the best, you see,
> Yet they've all read such a dreadful lot.
> How can we make it all seem fresh and new,
> Weighty, but entertaining too?
> -*Faust*, Part I: Prelude On Stage

I first discovered *Puella Magi Madoka Magica* (hereafter referred to as simply *Madoka Magica*) in August of 2014. I guess that makes me a pretty late arrival to the game, since the original series had been out for three years by that time. To be perfectly honest, I probably would never have discovered it had it not been for a specific set of circumstances. You see, even though I had been an avid consumer of anime since the late 1980s, I had never really been into the mahou shoujo (magical girl) genre. I generally stick to what I like, and I like sci-fi. I do regularly venture out from my sci-fi core, especially for anything by Hayao Miyazaki, or the occasional comedy, historical fiction or horror. Despite having watched hundreds of anime, I had never even finished a single episode of *Sailor Moon*. However, being an active member of the anime community for thirty plus years means you can't avoid picking up the basics of such a ubiquitous series. Still, I did love the *Tenchi Muyo* franchise, and therefore I had seen some *Magical Girl Pretty Sammy*, but that had more to do with my love for *Tenchi* than any interest in magical girl anime.

What caused me to watch *Madoka Magica*? The fact that I love meeting the people behind the anime as much as I enjoy watching it. I go to as many cons as I can possibly make it to, and I have made some good friends in the industry. So, in the fall of 2014 I just happened to be in Albuquerque, New Mexico, and the University of New Mexico was putting on a con just minutes from where I was staying. Of course I planned to attend, and the guest of honor was Christine Marie Cabanos, the voice actress who played Madoka in the English dub of the series. I wanted to be familiar with her work when I met her, so I decided to watch the *Madoka Magica* series.

Two episodes in, I was completely unimpressed. I couldn't understand the reason for all the critical acclaim for the series. It seemed completely formulaic and cliché. Little did I know that I had just fallen for a carefully planned and executed trap; a trap laid by the series creators to lull the audience into a false sense of security. The first two episodes of the series were purposefully drawn and advertised to appear as a typical, happy go lucky, magical girl anime, and fully intended to play into the audiences expectations.

Then came the infamous third episode. I know I'm supposed to make a joke about Mami Tomoe losing her head at this point, but I once unintentionally made a Mami cosplayer cry by doing that, so I will refrain (much like the show, she was just playing with my emotions). The reality of being a magical girl went from glamorous, to dangerous, to a fate worse than death. First Mami dies, then we find out that Kyoko, the girl we love to hate, is actually a tragic character whose father killed the rest of her family before committing suicide, making you feel like an ass for having hated her. Then Sayaka gives in to despair when she realizes she sold her soul for a boy who ends up with another girl. Kyoko gives her own life to end Sayaka's suffering. The cute little bunny-cat ends up being a soul eating devil. And episode ten all but demands that you watch the entire series over again now that you know what's actually going on, and all you can do is say "Yes sir, Mr. Urobuchi, I'll get right on that as soon as I get back from buying another box of tissues."

To call it an emotional rollercoaster is perhaps an understatement. It's more like taking a dive into the deep end of a chilly pool of despair and feeling the relief when you surface and take a breath of fresh air supplied by the series' hopeful ending. Why take that plunge again? Because that pool of despair also contains heroism and true selflessness, love, and the indefatigable will to fight against impossible odds to save that which matters more than life itself. It's a wild ride through unfamiliar territory.

After thirty years of watching anime, I thought I had just about seen it all. Sure, there was new stuff every year, and some of it quite good, but for the most part they followed a fairly predictable pattern of success copying. I really didn't think anything could surprise me anymore. *Madoka Magica* did. That it contrasted a fairly dark, very serious plot against colorful, happy imagery surprised me, but not as much as the sheer depth of the writing. That a magical girl anime could bring a tear to this grown man's eye, now that was surprising!

The story was like an onion. Peel back a layer and you just find another layer. I have had favorite shows before that I would watch again and again, but this was different. I was re-watching it not just because I enjoyed it (which I did), but because I was studying it. There were themes within themes; religious themes, themes from classical literature and legend, and conceptual themes of balance and selflessness, love, hope and despair. The visual metaphors and symbolism of Gekidan Inu Cury's imagery are enough to write a whole book on. My efforts to get to the bottom of all this will doubtless go on for years.

The following is an incomplete work. I will continue to study my favorite work of fiction, as well as any future offerings this franchise produces, long after this book is published. I'm sure this will be one of my favorite pastimes for the foreseeable future, and one I thoroughly enjoy. But what is the point of studying something if you aren't going to share what you find? So here it is. This book is a collection of observations on *Puella Magi Madoka Magica*, presented in an academic yet hopefully entertaining format, for the purpose of critique, and as a milestone of my understanding of these works of fiction so that I might build upon that foundation with future commentary. I hope you enjoy it.

Introduction

This book is not intended to be used as a reference, like a dictionary or an encyclopedia. It is not organized in a way that will allow you to watch *Madoka Magica*, book in hand, and look up whatever symbol or nuance you encounter. Rather it is meant to be read in its entirety, after at least one full viewing of either the original series, or the two recap movies, and most importantly *Rebellion*. If you have not seen any one of these, read no further, as the contents will make little sense to you, and you will encounter unforgiveable spoilers.

The *Magica Quartet* seem to be obsessed with extremely long titles. For the purposes of this book I have reduced the names of these titles. When the term *Madoka Magica* is used, it refers to the *Puella Magi Madoka Magica* franchise as a whole, not just the TV series, which will be referred to as 'the original series.' *Madoka Magica the Movie One: Beginnings Story, Madoka Magica the Movie Two: Eternal Story, and Madoka Magica the Movie Three: Rebellion Story*, will be called simply *Beginnings, Eternal,* and *Rebellion.*

This book is primarily aimed at the American, or at least the English speaking audience of *Madoka Magica.* This is because I am a native English speaker, and although I do speak a fair amount of Japanese, and watch the show as much in Japanese as I do in English, I am nevertheless geographically challenged. By this I mean that I live in America, and therefore I have greater access to the American anime industry, i.e. the English voice cast and crew. As much as I would love to have interviewed Gen Urobuchi for this project, or to have had the chance to speak with Chiwa Saito, my efforts to do so were fruitless. Nevertheless, I would like to point out that the English script adaptation was extremely faithful to the original Japanese story, and the performances of the English cast were, in my humble opinion, the equal of their Japanese counterparts. In some areas the English voice cast has benefitted from having seen the finished product before voicing the characters, giving them added insight into those characters.

I am a very active member of the US anime community, making it to more cons per year than all but the most in-demand voice actors and members of the industry. I have had the good fortune of making friends in the industry over the years, and I have leveraged those connections to improve this book by adding commentary from the cast and crew. My hope is that you, the reader, will get not only my take on the characters and story, but also the thoughts of those who brought those characters to life.

This book presents interpretations of the symbols, metaphors, literary references, and themes of *Madoka Magica*. It primarily covers the original series, the two recap movies *Beginnings* and *Eternal*, and the sequel movie *Rebellion*. It also includes some information from the manga, but that is not the focus of this work. The reason for the book is to aid viewers in getting more out of the viewing experience by giving a basic understanding of the subtext, and to foster a greater appreciation of the work. If you watch *Madoka Magica* and only see it as a somewhat dark magical girl story, then you have missed a great deal. One of the greatest aspects of these works of art is that their re-watch value is as high, or higher than the entertainment value of the original viewing.

This book will help the viewer peel away the layers of the onion to see the story beneath the surface. The story of *Madoka Magica* is like an iceberg. What you see on the surface is only the beginning. Particularly with *Rebellion*, the real meat of the tale is underneath, needing to be deciphered. However, this decryption need not be a laborious or tedious one. If research is something that you enjoy, then by all means do it. However, if you want the answers conveniently gift wrapped and handed to you, then this book is what you are looking for. Read this, then go back and re-watch the show, and see that there was another world lying just beneath the surface that you didn't see on the first viewing.

The Case for Faust

FAUST Still a document, written and signed,
That's a ghost makes all men fear it.
The word is already dying in the pen,
And wax and leather hold the power then.
What do you want from me base spirit?
Will iron: marble: parchment: paper do it?
Shall I write with stylus, pen or chisel?
I'll leave the whole decision up to you.

MEPHISTOPHELES Why launch into oratory too?
Hot-tempered: you exaggerate as well.
Any bit of paper's just as good.
And you can sign it with a drop of blood.

FAUST If it will satisfy you, and it should,
Then let's complete the farce in full.

-Faust, Part I Scene IV: The Study

Why start with *Faust*? Because of all the themes of the original series, it is the most overt. If you noticed any of the references to classic literature which saturate this series, the one you are most likely to pick up on is *Faust*. But was the series actually based on *Faust*? The series writer, Gen Urobuchi seems to suggest that it wasn't.

> Q: Madoka seems to be inspired by Goethe's *Faust* and in *Psycho-Pass* you quoted works from Max Weber and other German writers. How did you discover them and how did they inspire you?
>
> A: The designers from SHAFT thought of inserting the quotes from *Faust*. I only noticed them when people approached me asking about them. My main inspirations are eroge and classical literature.[1]
>
> - Nitro+ Q&A Panels at Animagic 2013

---

1. Gen Urobuchi, Nitro+ Q&A Panel at Animagic 2013, accessed 23 April 2015, http://wiki.puella-magi.net/Nitro%2B_Q%26A_Panels_at_Animagic_2013.

Yet the *Faust* references are hardly deniable. The basic resemblance which most people catch onto is the contract. Faust makes a deal with Mephistopheles (the devil), who is to be his servant for life, in return, if the devil is able to make Faust truly happy, the devil gets Faust's soul after he dies. Faust wishes for youth, and is transformed into a young man, falls in love with a girl named Gretchen, and of course it all ends in tragedy because any deal that sounds too good to be true, probably is.

To make the resemblance even stronger, the devil first appears to Faust as a dog, and only Faust can see the supernatural nature of the animal. This is of course similar to Kyubey, who is a small animal who can only be seen by magical girls and magical girl candidates, and pushes the girls into making a contract which ultimately costs them their souls.

In Part I, Scene II, of *Faust*, the titular character and his friend Wagner are out enjoying a festival when a black dog begins circling them, moving incrementally closer. Faust is certain he can see hints of flame as the animal moves, but Wagner sees nothing unusual about the dog. Faust takes the dog home with him, and later that night, it reveals itself to be Mephistopheles, and takes human form. In *Madoka Magica*, the idea that only the intended target can see the animal for what it is has been taken even farther, with Kyubey completely invisible to normal humans, even to the point of taking a bath in a bowl of water on the counter in front of both Madoka and her mom while they brush their teeth and get ready for the day ahead. Madoka's mom never notices Kyubey at all.

Also both stories show the intent of the one offering the contract to keep information from the one signing the contract. Kyubey only tells the girls they will get one wish, magical powers, and a life fighting witches if they sign the contract. He never mentions what he gets out of the deal, and of course the devil's in the details.

If only the magical girls had been as wise as old Faust, they could have avoided so much suffering. When the devil first proposes the contract, he wants to keep things vague, much like the way Kyubey hides the details of the contract from the girls. Faust knows better, and challenges the devil to spell out every detail of the agreement:

> FAUST And what must I do in exchange?
>
> MEPHISTOPHELES There's lots of time:
> you've got the gist.
>
> FAUST No, no! The Devil is an egotist,
> Does nothing lightly, or in God's name,
> To help another, so I insist,
> Speak your demands out loud,
> Such servants are risks, in a house.
>
> *Faust*, Part 1, Scene IV, The Study

Of course, the magical girls got the worse of the two deals. Faust gets the devil as a servant for life, and the devil only gets Faust's soul if the devil is able to make him completely happy. The magical girls are signing a contract for a life of servitude, fighting deadly battles against witches for their entire lives. They get powers, but at the cost of having their souls ripped from their bodies and placed inside a jewel, which turns darker whenever they use their powers, or feel despair. Eventually, perhaps unavoidably, once the gem becomes black, they transform into the very witches they have been fighting and are killed by other magical girls, possibly their own friends. This seems bad enough, until you realize that once the still living magical girls use up the last bit of the defeated witch's soul gem to cleanse their own, that gem, and the former magical girl's soul is then consumed by Kyubey.[2] So the only two possible outcomes of this contract are death in combat, or having your soul eaten by Kyubey. Anyone who says he's not evil should probably take another look at the deal he's selling.

But the magical girls get wishes, right? So they can potentially have anything they desire in exchange for this contract. Unfortunately, both *Madoka Magica* and *Faust* both subscribe to a similar theory; wishes ultimately betray the wisher. Kyubey spells this out in *Rebellion* when he says, "Oh no, we didn't betray them. You could say their wishes did

---

[2]. Kyubey demonstrates this to Sayaka. In her room, she uses the grief seed from Elly to purify her own soul gem (the last, possibly only, time she will do so), and Kyubey states that eating the blackened grief seeds is "one of my duties!" *Puella Magi Madoka Magica*, episode six, "This Just Can't be Right," 3:53.

though. Wishes are things which don't exist in the current reality, and anything that deviates from reality is bound to create a distortion. So why does it surprise anyone that these things end in disaster?" (Original Series, Episode 11, 18:50) And Faust sees a similar effect in his contract. Faust wants youth and love, but he is betrayed by his wish. He gets Mephistopheles to make him young again, and he falls in love with a young girl named Gretchen. He has Mephistopheles manipulate the situation to get Gretchen to reciprocate those feelings, but it all backfires. Gretchen's brother Valentine catches Faust wooing his sister and goes ballistic. He publicly proclaims Gretchen to be a whore, and starts a sword fight with Faust. Faust kills him in self defense and has to flee to avoid the authorities. Gretchen falls into despair from the loss of her brother, the disappearance of her lover (Faust), and the public humiliation she has just faced, making her a social outcast.

Gretchen's emotional disintegration is very *Madoka Magica*-esque. She falls apart about as quickly as Sayaka, heading down a path of intentional self destruction, and she ends up in prison charged with the death of her (and Faust's) baby. Sentenced to death, she accepts her fate, even to the point of refusing to go with Faust when he stages a rescue attempt. Again, much like Sayaka, Gretchen has completely given in to despair and no longer wants to live. Faust and Mephistopheles are forced to flee without saving her. Mephistopheles then takes Faust off to Walpurgis Night, a gathering and party for witches, in order to cheer him up. This is clearly the inspiration for the final witch of the series, Walpurgisnacht, who appears to be a conglomeration of multiple witches.

The early episodes of the series are littered with *Faust* quotes. They appear not only in runes inside the witches' labyrinths, but also in the original German as graffiti on walls outside the labyrinths. It's almost as if the show is trying to make sure you don't miss the literary connection.

If you needed any other convincing that *Madoka Magica* and *Faust* were related, just translate the on-screen runes which announce Madoka's witch form when she transforms in episode ten after defeating Walpurgisnacht. The runes name Madoka's witch form ᛕᚱᛁᛖᛗᚺᛁᛚᛞ ᚷᚱᛖᛏᚲᚺᛖᚾ, or "Kriemhild Gretchen."

So why, with all these similarities and overt references to *Faust* found in *Madoka Magica*, would Gen Urobuchi deny that he was inspired by *Faust*? There are really only three possibilities. First, he is being deceptive, and *Faust* was in fact an inspiration. Second, all these apparent *Faust* references are just coincidences. Or third, we have misinterpreted what he was saying in the interview.

We may never know whether or not Urobuchi was telling the truth in this interview. We do have reason to take his interview answers with a grain of salt. He has falsified his answers in the past. In fact, when it was revealed that he was the writer, he took to Twitter to do damage control. He was afraid that his reputation for writing dark and violent stories would give too much away about the true nature of *Madoka Magica*. Director Akiyuki Shinbo still wanted that to be a surprise, so he did his best to mislead his own fans.[3]

Still, he had good reason to deceive the public when he gave the above answer. The series producers were working hard to create a false image of the nature of the series, in order to enhance the surprise created when the story became dark. I can attest that having watched the series without any spoilers to ruin it, the surprise factor was a stroke of genius, and is probably responsible for a large portion of the show's renown and high reputation. However, with the answer to the *Faust* question, there doesn't seem to be any such reason for deceiving the public. The interview was done in 2013, and the cat was already out of the bag.

If he was telling the truth, then how do we explain so many *Faust* references in a story which the author denies was inspired by *Faust*? Could they really be coincidences? Of course it's possible. Other anime have involved a similar concept of a contract. *Darker Than Black* included contracts as a means of gaining powers, and the characters were even referred

---

3. Gen Urobuchi, "Ultra Creators Interview," *Ultra Jump EGG*, accessed 24 November 2015, https://wiki.puella-magi.net/Ultra_Jump_EGG_Urobuchi_Interview.

to as contractors. The names Walpurgisnacht and Kriemhild Gretchen may have been chosen by some other member of the team, and Urobuchi may not have been involved with that part of the creative process. After all, the witches and their labyrinths were designed by Inu Curry. He is probably telling the truth that the direct *Faust* quotes, seen as graffiti on various walls in the show, were added by the production team.

Still, there are just too many references for it to be a simple coincidence, and no apparent reason for a cover-up. However, that doesn't mean the writer himself was inspired by *Faust*. Other members of the team may have spotted the basic similarities in the premise, and enhanced the resemblance with names and quotations unintended by the author. This would seem to be what he was saying in his answer to the interview question, but maybe we are reading more into his answer than he intended.

On the first reading, his answer to the question about *Faust* would seem to indicate a denial, but let's take a closer look at the exact wording. He says, "The designers from SHAFT thought of inserting the quotes from *Faust*. I only noticed them when people approached me asking about them. My main inspirations are eroge and classical literature." If we break that down, we can actually read it to mean the opposite. First of all, he never directly denies *Faust* as an inspiration. He only says that he didn't notice the *Faust* quotes (appearing as graffiti), and that they were added by, "The designers from SHAFT," and not by himself, which is obviously true. He is a writer, not an animator. The backgrounds and scenery are designed by others, and therefore he may have disagreed with, or been unaware of, their insertion. He may simply be stating that he didn't mean for the *Faust* references to be so blatant, or 'in your face.' Additionally, he does say that he was primarily inspired by classic literature, and *Faust* is, of course, classic literature. The denial is implied, but never actually stated.

Let's compare this apparent denial to something more literal (or tangible), such as hiding Easter eggs (actual ones, not the kind you find in movies). In this case you have hidden a bunch of Easter eggs in your yard for your family and friends to hunt, and you did an awesome job of hiding them. However, one of your friends places a few eggs out where they are easily seen. The hunt begins, and one of the egg hunters picks up the easy to find eggs and comments that you didn't hide the eggs very well. To which you reply, "I didn't hide those eggs! When I hide eggs, they're hard to find!" By this you mean that you didn't hide the ones which your friend put out in the open, but it comes across like you are denying having hidden Easter eggs at all. Perhaps that's what has happened with Urobuchi's answer to the *Faust* question. It's just a misinterpretation of his comment.

If we remove the superfluous info about *Psycho Pass*, and the statement about the SHAFT inserted quotations, we are left with:

Q: *Madoka* seems to be inspired by Goethe's *Faust*...and other German writers.

How did you discover them and how did they inspire you?

A: ...My main inspirations are eroge and classical literature.

It's hard to read that any other way, now that the comment about the SHAFT inserted quotations have been omitted. So, to all of those bloggers and commentators out there who insist that Gen Urobuchi is overrated as a writer[4], and that we are seeing sophisticated inspiration where none exists[5], this author suggests that you should probably take another look at the evidence.

Of course, the helpful creature handing out magical powers is an element which appears not only in *Madoka Magica*, but in all magical girl anime, as it should. This is a leftover from the magical girl's origins as a young witch with a familiar (see chapter 10, Color Coded for Your Convenience). And the devil appearing as an animal in *Faust* is only a reference to that

---

4. According to *Anime Maru*, this actually led to his decision to retire from writing. The story was satirical, but still serves to point out the sheer volume of negative criticism aimed at Urobuchi, especially in the comments which follow the article. "Urobuchi Gen Retires After Receiving Internet Criticism," *Anime Maru*, (May 7, 2014), accessed 14 May 2015, http://www.animemaru.com/urobuchi-gen-retires-after-receiving-internet-criticism/

5. As with any creative work, much of Gen Urobuchi's writing has been criticized by fans (with whom this author does not agree). A quick google search reveals numerous blogs, reviews, and forums which feature claims that viewers are seeing a depth of writing which does not exist. A prime example is the *Youtube* anime reviewer Kevin Nyaa. "The Problems With: Madoka Magica Rebellion," *Youtube*, accessed 14 May 2015, https://www.youtube.com/watch?v=EEldbOjnn8s.

same tradition, the witch's familiar. So, to some extent, it is difficult to tell which elements of *Madoka Magica* are directly related to *Faust* and which elements share a common source which inspired both Urobuchi and Goethe.

Still, the evidence for a connection is overwhelming. *Madoka Magica* and *Faust* are most definitely related. Whether or not Gen Urobuchi specifically wrote in those similarities or if they were added by other members of the Magica Quartet team, they are there, they are intentional, and they are undeniable.

The Christian Perspective

Madoka, suspended before Homura's clockworks by the threads of karmic destiny. Her position is reminiscent of a crucifixion. (Original Series, Episode 11, 0:01:45).

Madoka Magica is not a Christian tale, to be sure. Nor is it a Buddhist tale, or a retelling of any of the classics. It does, however, borrow heavily from all of these sources. This chapter will look at those story elements which are drawn both from the Bible, and from related Christian literature.

Anime in general loves to depict Christian images and symbols. They love our Christian legends and monsters, especially vampires. For perhaps the best example of this, check out the anime *Trinity Blood*. But a story doesn't have to involve Vatican priests battling legions of vampires to be Christian in nature. It can be far more satisfying when these ideas are more subtle.

One has to remember that Japan's population is 84% Buddhist, 71% Shinto (there is some overlap in these categories), and only 2% Christian.[6] So, for them, Christian ideas and images are as exotic as Eastern ideas and religions are to us in the West. Also, considering

---

6. "The World Factbook," *Central Intelligence Agency*, accessed 14 May 2015, https://www.cia.gov/library/publications/the-world-factbook/geos/ja.html.

that the vast majority of the audiences in Japan are relatively unfamiliar (compared to a western audience) with the workings of Christian religion, the writers often play fast and loose with the details, often getting them wrong. Sometimes, especially when they don't get into the minute details of the religion, anime stories can successfully integrate Christian ideas to create themes which western audiences find familiar and engaging. Taking ideas from varied sources, incorporating them into an original story without resorting to a literal re-telling the source material, and getting the audience to actively think about those ideas, is where *Madoka Magica* excels.

    The most obvious place to start is with Madoka herself. You can draw several parallels between her story and that of Christ. The most overt similarity is her sacrifice at the end of the series. Christ died on the cross, his sacrifice providing a path to salvation for those who accept it. Madoka similarly sacrificed herself, to save all magical girls, past present and future, from their fate of transformation into witches. Both sacrifices bought salvation for a specific group. Christ's sacrifice, while available to anyone, is only received by those who accept it. Madoka did not save everyone, just the magical girls. Her wish only provided salvation from despair. Although the girls no longer transformed into witches, they still died, and the curses remained in the world and still had to be fought.

    There are more similarities just in the sacrifice itself. After three days Jesus rose again and visited with his disciples before ascending to heaven. Similarly, before Madoka ascended, she visited with her four closest friends, speaking with them one last time before she became the Law of Cycles. Finally, Madoka disappeared from the world, ascending to another plane of existence, perhaps existing as hope itself, appearing at the end of every magical girl's life to save them from their own despair, allowing them to die in peace and not transform into witches. Likewise, Christ ascended to an eternal existence offering salvation to all from heaven. "So then, after the Lord had spoken unto them, he was received up into heaven, and sat on the right hand of God."[7]

---

7. Mark 16:19 (King James Version).

This mirror image pattern of sacrifice, visitation, and ascendance is fairly strong evidence for a connection, but that is not the end of the similarities. Both Christ and Madoka are tempted by a powerful creature who would literally offer the world in exchange for their souls.

Christ was tempted by the devil himself. "Then Jesus was led up by the Spirit into the wilderness to be tempted by the devil."[8] He was tempted three times, and the last one sounds the most like our favorite *Madoka Magica* villain. "Again, the devil took him to a very high mountain and showed him all the kingdoms of the world and their splendor; and he said to him, 'All these I will give you, if you will fall down and worship me.' Jesus said to him, 'Away with you, Satan! For it is written, 'Worship the Lord your God and serve only him.' Then the devil left him, and suddenly angels came and waited on him."[9]

Kyubey gets to play the role of devil in two distinct ways. He is both Faust's Mephistopheles, offering wishes in exchange for eternal servitude, and Christ's Satan, tempting the great redeemer to stray from the path. It is amusing that Kyubey actually goes farther than either of the devil roles on which he is based. In neither *Faust* nor the Bible does the devil actually engineer the situation which he offers to solve, but Kyubey does.

Kyubey asked Madoka to make a contract several times during the series. After she was reluctant to accept the deal when it was first offered, he began to place her in situations which would tempt her to make a wish, brazenly admitting his plan on more than one occasion. You may remember the line, "I think it's good you're coming along with us. That way if we find ourselves in a bad spot, you'll be our trump card."[10] The first time Kyubey placed Madoka in a situation where she had to make a contract was when Mami was killed by Charlotte. In his defense, he probably didn't engineer that situation.

---

8. Matthew 4:1 (New Revised Standard Version)

9. Matthew 4:8-11 (New Revised Standard Version)

10. *Puella Magi Madoka Magica* (The Original Series), episode 5, "There's No Way I'll Ever Regret It," (0:15:56).

Mami was his strongest ally, the queen in his chess set, and it would have been illogical to trade her for Madoka at that point. Later, Kyubey knowingly pits Kyoko against Sayaka in order to tempt Madoka into making a contract. This is where he begins his new tactic of actively creating the situation which pressures Madoka to accept his offer. He even tells Madoka that she can reverse Sayaka's fate, and return her to a normal girl with her wish. When that fails, he leads Kyoko to believe that it is possible to save Sayaka after she has transformed into a witch, which fails resulting in the deaths of both Sayaka (now Oktavia) and Kyoko. Kyubey, in a rare moment of honesty, later admitted to Homura that despite what he had told Kyoko, it had never been possible for her to save Sayaka. He had engineered their deaths so that Homura would be the only magical girl left in Mitakihara. Kyubey makes it clear that Homura can never defeat Walpurgisnacht alone, and that she cannot turn back time again without harming Madoka, and the only way out is for Madoka to make a contract. Kyubey would make a magnificent chess master.

Despite all this, not everyone will see the similarities. Jed A. Blue has written a fascinating critical analysis of the *Madoka Magica* universe (series, movies, and manga). He discounts the Christian influence in *Madoka Magica*, seeing a story strongly influenced by Buddhist ideas. In his own words, "She [Madoka] is not a Christ-figure, suffering and dying as a way of absorbing the sins of others…She is egoless and transcendent, and thus cannot suffer."[11] However, despite Blue's statement to the contrary, it is revealed in the 'field of daisies' scene in *Rebellion* that Madoka does suffer. In that scene, Madoka had been trapped in Homura's witch labyrinth, and returned to her normal, magical, but still human self. Homura talks around the issue of Madoka's ascendance, Madoka says, "I'm not going anywhere, especially if it's so far away I couldn't see you again. I'd never do something like that… If I did anything that would make someone as strong as you cry like this, it would break my heart."

---

11. Jed A. Blue, *The Very Soil: An Unauthorized Critical Study of Puella Magi Madoka Magica*, (Eohippus Press, 2014), 70.

Homura then asks, "It would break your heart? Leaving us behind would hurt you that much?" Madoka answers, "Of course it would."[12]

Mr. Blue also comments on the names Madokami and Godoka, given to Madoka's ascended form by fans. Blue says, "Madokanon would be more appropriate, as she is more Bodhisattva than divinity." While there is a definite, maybe even intentional similarity to nirvana in the state which Madoka achieves after her ascendance, she is still unquestionably a literal savior. This is in direct contradiction to Mr. Blue's own assertion that, "Homura is a Christian (or, at least, attended a Christian school). Like Kyoko, she has absorbed the belief that it is possible for one person to save another – that there is something to be saved from, and somewhere to be saved to. It is a fundamentally dualistic proposition – here is bad, there is good. But as Kyubey has made clear with his talk of karmic balance, we are in a Buddhist world."[13]

Nevertheless, salvation is exactly what Madoka achieves at the end of the series. Despite the fact that Homura fails to save Madoka during the events of the series, her wish is ultimately granted and she does finally succeed in saving Madoka in the *Rebellion* movie. There will be more on this in the chapter on *Rebellion*. For now, let's stick with the religious references.

It is interesting to note that Kyoko Sakura is often seen eating or hoarding apples. Why this particular food? Because in the Christian tradition the apple signifies sin. It is used as a metaphor for the original sin of Adam and Eve eating from the tree of wisdom. In *Madoka Magica*, Kyoko and her father both commit sins. Deuteronomy 4:2 states, "Ye shall not add unto the word which I command you, neither shall ye diminish ought from it, that ye may keep the commandments of the LORD your God which I command you."(KJV) In

---

12. *Madoka Magica the Movie: Rebellion*, (1:04:13). This dialogue indicates that Madoka does suffer, at the very least from a broken heart. It also confirms Homura's suspicion that Madoka made her decision because Kyubey forced her hand, not because she wanted to form a contract. She would never have left her friends and family behind if there had been another way. Being separated from them is too painful.

13. Blue, 64.

Kyoko's own words, "...one day he started preaching stuff that wasn't in the Bible..." *Beginnings*, (1:38.07) So in changing his message from the existing scriptures to one more modern and accessible, Kyoko's father had broken this commandment. Hypocritically, Kyoko's father is angry at her because she is a magical girl, calling her a witch, when he is no less a sinner than she. Indeed, the Bible does prohibit the practice of magic, but there is a triple irony here. Kyoko's father, a sinner, accuses his daughter of the sin of witchcraft for using magic to get people to listen to his blasphemous sermons, while she risks her life to battle actual witches.

The *Rebellion* movie also contains some fascinating parallels to another Christian story. This time it is not the Bible, but a book inspired by a handful of verses from the Bible. Jed Blue astutely points out the similarities between Homura's plight in *Rebellion* and that of Lucifer in Milton's *Paradise Lost*.[14]

This time, Homura gets to play the devil. *Paradise Lost* elaborates on the story of Lucifer's rebellion against God, where he led one third of the angels in an attempt to depose God and take his place on the throne of heaven. Most westerners are familiar with this story, because they read *Paradise Lost* as part of an English Literature class. The actual verses in the Bible which deal with this rebellion are found in Isaiah and Revelations, with the following being the most pertinent to the *Rebellion* movie:

> How art thou fallen from heaven, O Lucifer, son of the morning! How art thou cut down to the ground, which didst weaken the nations!
>
> For thou hast said in thine heart, I will ascend into heaven, I will exalt my throne above the stars of God: I will sit also upon the mount of the congregation, in the sides of the north:
>
> I will ascend above the heights of the clouds; I will be like the most High.
>
> Yet thou shalt be brought down to hell, to the sides of the pit.

---

14. Blue, 122.

They that see thee shall narrowly look upon thee, and consider thee, saying, Is this the man that made the earth to tremble, that did shake kingdoms;

That made the world as a wilderness, and destroyed the cities thereof; that opened not the house of his prisoners?[15]

The verse in Isaiah describes Lucifer's failed attempt to depose God, after which he and the angels who followed him were cast out of heaven; fallen angels, also known as demons. Homura is pictured at the end of the original series as a kind of champion of the goddess-like Madoka, remaining behind, fighting to protect the world which Madoka sacrificed herself for. In this scene, she has white, angel like wings, and carries Madoka's weapon.[16] She seems to have taken on the role of an arch angel, like Michael. To further drive home the metaphor, she is even given an added scene in *Eternal* where she sits among several graves and statues; one of these statues is the arch angel Michael. When asked about Homura's position at the end of the work, Gen Urobuchi described her as "an evangelist who is the only person within the world she lives in who understands Madoka's existence and role."[17]

Homura with angel-like wings descends to do battle with the wraiths after Madoka's ascension. (Original Series, Episode 12, 0:21:12)

15. Isaiah 14:12-17, (King James Version).

16. The bow wielded by Homura at the end of the original series may not be Madoka's. The design is different, and in episode one she can be clearly seen firing some type of purple energy blasts at Kyubey as he runs away. We never see the weapon which fired the purple energy, but Homura's bow is the only weapon we ever see her hold which is capable of this, indicating that she had it the whole time.

17. Ko Ransom, "Nico Character Chat with Kazuo Koike and Gen Urobuchi," *ANN*, (29 Jan 2012), accessed 10 Jan 2016, www.animenewsnetowrk.com/feature/2012-01-29

Like Lucifer, Homura will not remain an angel, but will lead a rebellion (thus the name of the film) against Madoka, deposing her from her position in heaven, which will result in Homura's fall from her position as Madoka's arch angel, and transformation into a demon.

Whether the story is inspired by the actual Bible, or from the classic literature which Gen Urobuchi loves so much, we may never know, but the similarities are undeniable. To his credit, Urobuchi has not simply re-told the story. He has taken it as inspiration, and made it his own. In the *Madoka Magica* story, the rebellion is successful. For how long remains to be seen. *Revelations* offers us a glimpse into the War in Heaven, where the angels of God battle and defeat the forces of Lucifer.

Madoka in the music shop. The poster on the wall forshadows the fallout from *Rebellion*. (*Beginnings* 0:12:45.)

Promotional poster for *Rebellion* featuring demon Homura.

> And there was war in heaven: Michael and his angels fought against the dragon; and the dragon fought and his angels,
>
> And prevailed not; neither was their place found any more in heaven.
>
> And the great dragon was cast out, that old serpent, called the Devil, and Satan, which deceiveth the whole world: he was cast out into the earth, and his angels were cast out with him.18

It's a pretty safe bet that a sequel to *Rebellion* will be made, and an equally safe bet that we will see this war in heaven, with the magical girls playing the angels in this supernatural conflict. This is made all the more apparent by Homura's final conversation with Madoka at the end of the movie. Homura says, "I see. Well then. I suppose one day you will also be my enemy."(*Rebellion*, 1:48:43)

---

18. Revelations 12:7-9, (King James Version).

The Undiscovered Country
Death and Despair in *Madoka Magica*

One of the many images of suicide which pervade *Madoka Magica*. (*Rebellion*, 1:25:38)

Is *Madoka Magica* a dark story? Some, such as Chuck Sonnenburg, one of my favorite critics, insist that *Madoka Magica* is not dark. Sonnenburg states in his reviews that the story does contain dark elements, but focuses on the fight to overcome that darkness.[19] While that is true, it all comes down to your definition of dark. The *Merriam-Webster Dictionary* defines dark (as it applies to a subject matter) as, "relating to grim or depressing circumstances <dark humor>."[20] *Wise Geek*, a website dedicated to answering common questions, describes dark fiction as, "a genre of fiction concerned with fear, death, and the sinister side of human nature."[21] *Madoka Magica* easily fits into either of these two descriptions.

19. Chuck Sonnenburg, "An Opinionated Look at: Madoka Magica Episode 4," *SF Debris*, accessed 16 June 2015. http://sfdebris.com/videos/anime/madoka4.php.

20. *Merriam-Webster Dictionary*, accessed 16 June 2015, http://www.merriam-webster.com/dictionary/dark.

21. "What is Dark Fiction?," *Wise Geek*, accessed 16 June 2015, http://www.wisegeek.com/what-is-dark-fiction.htm.

Homura feigns suicide to gain an edge in her fight with Mami. Although she knows she will survive so long as her soul gem is intact, the look on her face is convincing. (*Rebellion*, 0:51:35)

Death and depression are center stage in *Madoka Magica*. The true battle isn't against the witches, but an internal struggle as the magical girls fight their inevitable descent into despair. This is most clearly shown in the Sayaka story arc. This is a girl who, in episode two, pointed out how she had such a good life that she couldn't think of anything to wish for. However, by episode eight, she is in such emotional pain that she lashes out at her best friend, possibly even kills two strangers on a train, and eventually is consumed by despair and transforms into a witch; a thinly veiled metaphor for ending her own life. In fact, only one of the five magical girls does not at least attempt to commit suicide at some point.

It can be difficult to understand suicide. There are many theories and explanations out there. While there are certainly many reasons why someone would wish to end their own life, **pain**, is the reason most germane to *Madoka Magica*. What follows is the author's view on the issue, and he is by no means a professional.

Most people can comprehend why an individual who has been horribly injured, far from

Homura, crying spider web tears. Simultaneously a symbol of her pain, and the trap she is setting to catch the unsuspecting Madoka. (*Rebellion*, 1:19:37)

help and in incredible pain, would end their own life to stop the physical suffering. Physical pain is a sensation that we are all familiar with, and it is easy to understand how someone could be in so much anguish that they would rather die. Emotional pain, or at least extreme emotional pain, is something most people are far less familiar with. But anyone who has actually been there knows that it can hurt just as intensely as the physical variety, and the greater the pain, the more desperate the need for a solution. Both types of injuries need treatment, but the nature of depression is such that we cannot see anything but our current circumstances. Imagine breaking your arm, and absolutely believing that it will continue to hurt like that for the rest of your life. That is what our mind can trick us into believing when we have been emotionally injured, but of course it isn't true. *Madoka Magica* shows us characters in this kind of emotional pain, and their battle to overcome despair is the central conflict which drives the story.

Rebellion portrays this psychological battle in its own unique artistic style. The scene at 1hr 24min shows Homulilly, Homura's witch form, shackled, her head broken, crowned with red spider lilies, being led off to the guillotine by an army of her familiars. In Japan, the red spider lily is associated with funerals and death. Her head is broken, not only a reference to the *Nutcracker*, whose jaw was broken rendering it useless for cracking nuts, but also a visual metaphor for her own feelings of worthlessness at having failed to save Madoka. From her back protrudes a phonograph speaker, symbolizing how her life has been a broken record, repeating the same tragic events over and over. She goes willingly to her execution, but part of her still clings to the desire to live. The ribbons on the back of her dress turn into giant arms, grabbing at buildings and tearing the city apart in a vain attempt to stop her determined march to death.

Homulilly. (*Rebellion*, 1:25:37)

Even if we only count the main characters (including Hitomi), the show contains five suicides or attempted suicides. That is, if we count Sayaka's transformation into a witch as a suicide. This is included in the total because Sayaka deliberately followed a self-destructive path of fighting without cleansing her soul gem, rejecting help. Based on comments she made it is almost certain that she expected to die as a result. Other than her, we have Kyoko's suicide when she destroys her own soul gem to end Sayaka's suffering. Let's not make the mistake of thinking that Kyoko had to die at that point. She could have fled, and returned with Homura to put Sayaka down. Kyoko was profoundly lonely, and scarred by the belief that she was responsible for the death of her own family.

Sayaka had awakened in Kyoko those lost feelings of heroism and a love of fairy tale endings. She saw Sayaka as her ticket out of loneliness and hopelessness. Losing her was the straw that broke the camel's back. There is also Madoka, who doesn't technically take her own life, but enlists Homura to assist her suicide by shooting her soul gem in order to prevent her from becoming a witch. Hitomi joins a suicidal cult, but is saved by Madoka. And finally, nearly the entire third act of the *Rebellion* movie is concerned with Homura's desire to end her own life in order to thwart Kyubey's plans, and because she cannot live without Madoka.

The story doesn't stop there, in addition to the pervasive theme of suicide, the characters do kill each other off for various reasons. The magical girl fratricide rate is quite alarming. Kyoko attempts to murder Sayaka in order to take her territory. Homura, in order to prevent Madoka from getting hurt, would surely have killed Sayaka in cold blood

Kyoko and Homura deliver the lifeless body of Sayaka to her best friend, Madoka. (*Eternal*, 0:06:25)

had Kyoko not stopped her. And in an alternate timeline, Mami kills Kyoko upon learning that all magical girls eventually become witches. She would have killed Homura next, but she underestimated Madoka, who shot and killed her before she could finish off the already restrained Homura.

Of all the characters, which one causes more death than any other? It would be tempting to say Kyubey, since anyone making a contract with him will die, either by a witch or at the hands of other magical girls. But it is Madoka, who uses her bow in the final, climactic battle at the end of *Rebellion* to exterminate the Incubators on their home world (except for at least one individual, fittingly enslaved by Homura). Not that Madoka wasn't justified. After all, these creatures have been preying on unsuspecting girls since prehistoric times, and have demonstrated that they will kill every last human being to attain their goal.[22] They may not have understood the suffering they were causing, but they clearly knew that they were causing it. One does not need to understand how they are hurting someone else in order to comprehend that it is wrong. The heat death of the universe is billions of years away, this isn't exactly an emergency. Maybe they could take a couple hundred million years to think about it. They might just come up with another way to fix it that doesn't involve sacrificing children.

A chapter on the theme of death in *Madoka Magica* wouldn't be complete without mentioning her. Mami Tomoe was the first major character to die in the show. Her death was the turning point at which the show stopped pretending to be something that it wasn't, and started to show its true face. Gen Urobuchi has a reputation for killing off characters, which earned him the nickname Urobutcher. But he isn't just killing off characters randomly, or on a whim. Death is used to enhance the story. Mami's death was used to up the stakes and demonstrate the true dangers involved in being a magical girl. More importantly, it followed a familiar pattern of allowing the mentor to introduce the hero to the new world, but removing that mentor before the hero was fully prepared. You might recognize this pattern from *The Lord of the Rings*, where Gandolf, mentor to Frodo, was killed during *The Fellowship of the Ring*. Gandolf was resurrected later, but his early death had the intended effect. The death of Obi Wan Kenobi in *Star Wars* bears an uncanny resemblance to Mami Tomoe's demise. Like Mami, Obi Wan was just starting to introduce Luke to the ways of the Jedi when he, like Mami, literally lost his head. In anime, a famous example is *Super Dimension Fortress Macross*, and *Robotech: The Macross Saga*. Roy Fokker was the mentor, and a much loved character among fans.

Roy's early death in *Robotech* announced to American audiences of the 1980s that this was no ordinary cartoon they were watching. For many, this author included, it was their first exposure to anime and the death of a major character was a bold statement that this was a

---

22. In episode 10, and *Eternal*, Kyubey states that Madoka will eventually become the most powerful witch ever. When this happens, he predicts that she will destroy the planet within ten days, and then adds, "It's humanity's problem now." *Eternal*, (0:53:35).

story with high stakes. It is difficult to estimate just how influential the death of Roy Fokker was to the formation of anime fandom, and the anime industry in America.

Mami doesn't really come off as a terribly tragic character, but there's more to her tragedy than is apparent at first, and like most, that centers around death. In this case, it is death that she could have prevented, but her haste cost the lives of her family and doomed her to a life of servitude without payment. Mami's suggestion that Madoka wish for a giant cake seems ridiculous at first, but not if we consider Mami's own wish. In a scene from the original series, which was unfortunately cut from the *Beginnings* movie, Mami was fatally wounded in a car crash, and Kyubey offered to save her life if she became a magical girl. An offer she truly couldn't refuse. Her wish, as far as we know, was to live. Since she lives alone, we also presume that she was so hasty when she made her wish that she forgot to include her parents in that wish. It would have to be difficult living with the knowledge that you had the power to save your parents, but due to your own hasty decision, they died anyway. That would be bad enough, but we haven't reached rock bottom yet. If Mami's wish truly was to save her own life, then she in effect forfeited her wish entirely. A magical girl can heal her own body with magic, like Homura does when she heals her own eyes so that she no longer needs glasses. Also, a magical girl cannot die of physical injuries. Only the destruction of her soul gem can kill a magical girl. No matter what Mami had wished for, she would have lived. As soon as the contract was made, she would have received her soul gem, and effectively become immortal. Had she wished for anything, a penny, or perhaps even a cake, she would have gotten her life, and her wish. She might as well have said, "never mind the wish, just make me a magical girl." In light of that, her recommendation that Madoka make a wish for a giant cake is infinitely better than the wish she made for herself. Coincidentally, a cake is precisely what Charlotte, or rather Nagisa, the magical girl who would later become Charlotte, wished for.[23]

It is ironic that Mami, who had counseled Madoka and Sayaka against making

---

23. Production notes reveal that in exchange for making a contract, Charlotte recieved precisely "one-whole cheesecake...My dying mother wanted to eat it. But, perhaps, I should have cured her disease instead. However, that surely wasn't appropriate." *Puella Magi Production Notes*, (Japan: SHAFT, 2011), 120.

a hasty wish, would suddenly change course and start pressuring Madoka to make a wish. When Mami and Madoka enter Charlotte's labyrinth, not only does Mami make the ridiculous suggestion about wishing for a cake, but she pushes Madoka to come up with a wish by the time Charlotte has been defeated. This almost irreconcilable change in her character could even be seen as a betrayal. Mami knows the consequences of making a hasty wish, and still pushes Madoka to do the same, reinforcing the fact that Mami has always been a pawn of Kyubey. He wants Madoka to make a contract, the sooner the better. It is poetic justice, or perhaps karma, that Mami died immediately after this betrayal.[24]

Death, when used appropriately, can create a strong bond between the audience and the character. When we know that our favorite character truly might not make it to the end of the series, we feel the tension in the story all the more strongly, and begin to worry about the fate of our favorites in a much different way than in a story where the hero has powerful plot armor. The importance of maintaining this sense of peril is pointed out by the writer himself when director Akiyuki Shinbo got so attached to Sayaka that he asked Urobuchi to bring her back to life after her death in episode nine. Urobuchi stood his ground, pointing out that her death was essential to the story, and bringing her back would cause too many problems.[25] The rules of this fictional universe had been established, and to break them would remove the tension which he had been carefully building in the narrative.

In the same way that Mami's death upped the stakes by letting the audience know just how dangerous the witches could be, Sayaka's death served to inform us of what happens to those magical girls who do not die in combat. With her transformation into a witch, it becomes clear to the audience that the contract Kyubey is offering is an inescapable death sentence. Not only that, but Sayaka's story arc shows us just how

---

24. Originally pointed out by a panelist at Con Jikan, Albuquerque NM, 1 Nov 2014. Panel name: "Madoka Magicanalysis: The Hero's Journey." Panelist name unknown.

25. "Interview with Gen Urobuchi," *Shinjidai no Mixture Magazine BLACK PAST*, (June 2011), translated by user symbv from evageeks forum, accessed 17 June 2015, https://wiki.puella-magi.net/Shinjidai_no_Mixture_Magazine_BLACK_PAST.

quickly a girl can succumb to despair if she doesn't cleanse her soul gem. It's a perfect trap. Choosing not to fight, or simply ignoring the contract and living a normal life probably isn't an option. Homura states unequivocally that simply controlling your own body uses a small amount of energy, thus slowly tainting the gem. Even if this were not the case, a person can't be happy all the time (unless that was their wish) and negative feelings would accumulate in the gem, tainting it over time.

Mami's wish was to live, and fittingly, she is the only magical girl who never attempts suicide. Still, the point is that death, in one form or another is a central theme of *Madoka Magica*. Jed Blue, while not directly speculating on the mental state of writer Gen Urobuchi, at least infers that he may be giving the audience a glimpse into his troubled soul.[26] But as he himself has told us, classic literature is a primary influence in his writing. Nothing could be more classic than Shakespeare.

It's apparent that *Hamlet* was a strong influence on Urobuchi's writing, especially in the original series or the first two movies. There are strong ties between characters and themes in *Madoka Magica* and the play *Hamlet*. Both are preoccupied with death and suicide. Who doesn't know the famous "To be or not to be" soliloquy? Hamlet himself, distraught after the loss of his father, contemplates the idea of death throughout the play. Ophelia, after losing her father, gives in to despair and drowns herself. The strongest resemblance is that between Kyoko and Ophelia.

Both Kyoko and Ophelia are orphans. Kyoko's father killed the rest of her family and then himself. Ophelia's father was accidentally killed by Hamlet, and we never see any mother. Depending on your interpretation, you can say that both Kyoko and Ophelia have a love interest. Ophelia has Hamlet, and Kyoko… seems very fond of Sayaka. Both have a scene where they offer something to their love interest only to have the offering rejected. Kyoko offers an apple to Sayaka, a very meaningful gift coming from a girl with an intense eating

26. Blue, 28.

disorder and violent hatred of wasting food. Sayaka throws the apple on the ground. In Act 3 Scene 1, Ophelia tries to give Hamlet "certain remembrances," but Hamlet claims that he never loved her and similarly rejects the gifts. Of course, the stories of both Ophelia and Kyoko end in suicide.

Even their suicides have coincidences. Both involved mermaids. Kyoko died destroying Sayaka's witch form, Oktavia von Seckendorff, which appeared as an armored mermaid. Why a mermaid? Because Sayaka's story arc coincides very closely with Hans Christian Anderson's *The Little Sea Maid*.[27] When Queen Gertrude announces Ophelia's death, she says, "When down her weedy trophies and herself fell in the weeping brook. Her clothes spread wide; and, mermaid-like, awhile they bore her up: Which time she chanted snatches of old tunes; As one incapable of her own distress, or like a creature native and indued unto that element: but long it could not be till that her garments, heavy with their drink, pull'd the poor wretch from her melodious lay to muddy death."[28] In the *Rebellion* movie, Sayaka is "like a creature native and indued unto that element." She is able to summon her witch form whenever she is near water.

But what about Kyoko's family? Ophelia's father did not kill himself, or the rest of her family. Still, there is a scene in Hamlet which might fit the pattern. Hamlet's step father, Claudius, in a plot to poison Hamlet during the duel at the end of the play, ends up accidentally poisoning Queen Gertrude, Hamlet's mother. In the end, Hamlet, his mother Gertrude, Ophelia's brother Laertes, and Claudius himself die of the poison. This final scene is a fairly close fit to a father killing the rest of his family and himself. It's at least possible that it was a part of the inspiration for Kyoko's family history.

27. This relationship between Sayaka and *The Little Mermaid* is explored in detail in chapter four of this book.

28. William Shakespeare, *Hamlet*, "Act 4, Scene 7," accessed 10 January, 2016. http://shakespeare.mit.edu/hamlet/full.html.

If you needed any further evidence that there was a connection between *Madoka Magica* and *Hamlet*, look no further than the witches. The first witch killed by Mami was named Gertrud, same as Hamlet's mother. Even though she never became a witch during the events of the series, players of the PSP game *Puella Magi Madoka Magica Portable* know that Kyoko Sakura's witch form is named Ophelia.

Ophelia, Kyoko Sakura's witch form. Image source: *Puella Magi Wiki*. Accessed 17 June 2015. http://wiki.puella-magi.net/Ophelia.

To be, or not to be, that is the question:
Whether 'tis nobler in the mind to suffer
The slings and arrows of outrageous fortune,
Or to take arms against a sea of troubles
And by opposing end them. To die—to sleep,
No more; and by a sleep to say we end
The heart-ache and the thousand natural shocks
That flesh is heir to: 'tis a consummation
Devoutly to be wish'd. To die, to sleep;
To sleep, perchance to dream—ay, there's the rub:
For in that sleep of death what dreams may come,
When we have shuffled off this mortal coil,
Must give us pause—there's the respect
That makes calamity of so long life.
For who would bear the whips and scorns of time,
Th'oppressor's wrong, the proud man's contumely,
The pangs of dispriz'd love, the law's delay,
The insolence of office, and the spurns
That patient merit of th'unworthy takes,
When he himself might his quietus make
With a bare bodkin? Who would fardels bear,
To grunt and sweat under a weary life,
But that the dread of something after death,
The undiscovere'd country, from whose bourn
No traveller returns, puzzles the will,
And makes us rather bear those ills we have
Than fly to others that we know not of?
Thus conscience does make cowards of us all,
And thus the native hue of resolution
Is sicklied o'er with the pale cast of thought,
And enterprises of great pitch and moment
With this regard their currents turn awry
And lose the name of action.

Hamlet, Act 3 Scene 1.

The Mermaid and the Nutcracker

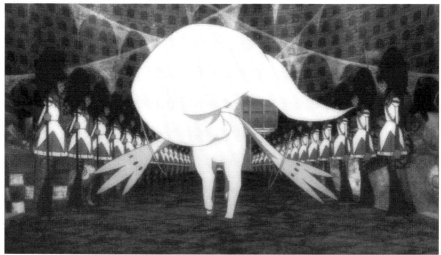

Kyubey plays the Mouse King to Homura's Nutcracker. (*Rebellion*, 1:11:44)

This chapter will be an exploration of metaphoric relationships of the major characters to their literary counterparts, with the exception of *Faust*, because that was given its own chapter. Not only will this be an exploration of the literary inspirations for all the major characters, but it will also explore some of the visual symbols which relate to those literary origins. In short, this chapter is about who the characters are, what may have inspired them, and how they are represented.

The Mermaid

Sayaka Miki is the most straightforward of the five girls to decipher. She is surrounded by symbols of knights, music, water, and sadness. Her color, blue, is fitting as she is overcome by melancholy faster than any of the other magical girls. Her witch form, Oktavia von Seckendorff, is a suit of medieval armor with a mermaid tail, in a labyrinth resembling a concert hall. Oktavia's weapon is the sword, oddly held in the left hand, despite the fact that Sayaka is right handed.

Why is Oktavia left handed? Probably because Sayaka's wish healed Kyosuke's left hand, the hand he holds his violin with. Like most of her concert hall like labyrinth, this is a reference to her wish. Ironically, and almost certainly intentionally so, Kyoko cuts off Oktavia's hand during her ill fated attempt to save her.

Sayaka has fallen for Mami Tomoe's vision of the magical girl as a powerful heroine, defender of the weak and champion of justice. Mami makes the job look flashy and glamorous, as well as noble. Sayaka of her own admission needs nothing. She has no idea what to wish for, because her life is basically a happy, comfortable one. Nevertheless, she wants to make a contract. She wants to be like Mami. She envisions herself as a knight, dedicated to a life of

Oktavia von Seckendorff, Sayaka's witch form. Notice the upper half combining a Knight and Orchestra Director, while the lower half consists of a mermaid tail. (*Eternal* 24:57)

valor, honor and justice, and that is reflected in her witch form.

But the knight and musical imagery are only the upper body of the witch. The lower body is a mermaid's tail. While the *Faust* references in *Madoka Magica* are some of the most overt, and certainly the most noticeable, Sayaka's relation to Hans Christian Anderson's *The Little Sea Maid* is the story arc with the most direct and strongest correlations of any of the characters in *Madoka Magica*. Please note that I am not referring to the animated Disney movie, *The Little Mermaid*, which was based on Anderson's work. There are significant differences between the Disney and Anderson versions.

Sayaka and *The Little Sea Maid* are almost the exact same story, just in a different setting. If you separate the knight and justice references, which are unique to Sayaka, the rest of the story and imagery bear a striking resemblance.

The little Sea Maid lives a happy and comfortable life as daughter of the Sea King. One day she ventures up to see the world above, and witnesses a Prince on his ship. A storm comes, and the Prince ends up in the water where he surely would have drowned had the Mermaid not saved him and taken him to land. Unfortunately, he is unconscious and does not witness his rescue, and never knows that it was the little Sea Maid who had saved him. When he awakes, he sees a girl on the beach, who is obviously a student at the nearby temple, and assumes she had pulled him from the sea.

Sayaka's witch form as it appeared in *Rebellion*. She has traded her sword for Kyoko's spear. This image clearly shows the mermaid tail. Source: *Rebellion* collector's edition box set booklet.

The Mermaid makes a deal with the Sea Witch, trading her voice for legs. The catch is that she must convince the Prince to marry her, or she will dissolve into sea foam. Of course, without a voice she cannot tell the Prince that it was she who had saved him. All is going well until the Prince finally finds the girl from the beach. She turns out to be a princess from a neighboring kingdom and of course the Prince marries her. The Mermaid returns to the sea, as foam.

Both characters fall in love with a boy whom they have saved. In both cases, that boy never knows that he was saved by the girl, or what the girl has sacrificed for him. Finally, in both stories the boy ends up with a different girl, and the heroine perishes as a tragic result.

The little Sea Maid even resembles Sayaka physically. While it is never stated what color her hair is, Anderson does describe her as having eyes, "blue as the deepest sea."[29] She also has an affinity for the colors blue and red. Her garden is filled with bright red and dark blue flowers.[30] It is hard to read this passage and not think of the image of Sayaka and Kyoko's blue and red

Sayaka's and Kyoko's silhouettes intermingled during the scene where Kyoko sacrifices herself to destroy Sayaka's witch form. (Episode 9, 20:22)

silhouettes swirling around each other when Kyoko sacrifices herself to end Sayaka's existence as a witch. Unfortunately, this image only appears in the TV version of the story, and was cut from the *Eternal* movie.[31]

The fact that the Sea Maid has no soul is a central point of the Anderson tale, and Urobuchi uses Sayaka as his means to express the idea that the magical girls have had their souls removed and placed in gems. It is Sayaka's soul gem which Madoka throws off the bridge, causing Sayaka's lifeless body to collapse until the gem is returned. Also, it is Sayaka whose soulless body is kept fresh by Kyoko's magic after she retrieves it from Oktavia's labyrinth. Anderson says of mermaids that they dissolve into sea foam at the end of their lives, and never have a grave. Ironically, Sayaka is the only magical girl to get a funeral, because the rest die in labyrinths and their bodies are never recovered.

Both Sayaka and the little Sea Maid make contracts with supernatural beings. Of

---

29. Hans Christian Anderson, *The Little Sea-Maid*, (Harvard Classics), accessed 15 December 2016, http://www.bartleby.com/17/3/4.html.

30. Ibid, 5.

31. This image was likely cut because the silhouettes appear to be nude. All scenes involving nudity were either cut from the movie versions, or re-drawn to give the characters clothes. This may have been a concession to make the movies more appropriate for western audiences' sensibilities, especially considering the age of the characters.

course Sayaka trades her soul to Kyubey and pledges herself to a life of fighting witches in exchange for healing the hand (why not his legs too?) of her beloved Kyosuke. The little Sea Maid trades her voice to the Sea Witch for legs so she can pursue her Prince on land, hoping to win his love and earn a soul. The fact that Sayaka almost never speaks to Kyosuke after making her contract is a fantastic similarity to Sea Maid's inability to speak to her Prince.

It is very likely that Kyosuke was Hitomi's secret admirer. This is paralleled in the Anderson story in that the Prince in the *Little Sea Maid* also had a love interest. When he awakened on the shore after being saved from drowning by the Sea Maid, he saw a beautiful girl with whom he instantly fell in love, and mistakenly believed she was the one who had saved him. He believed she was unavailable due to living in a temple, and resigned himself to the belief that he would never see her again. He later traveled to a neighboring country and found that the girl was only studying at the temple, but was actually the princess he was arranged to marry. This spelled death for the little Sea Maid, who would die if the Prince married anyone but her. After Sayaka used her wish to heal Kyosuke, he was released from the hospital, and despite knowing full well that Sayaka was in love with him (who could possibly miss this fact?) he agreed to be Hitomi's boyfriend when she asked him. This makes sense only if he already had an interest in her, and it also parallels the *Little Sea Maid* story, where the Prince immediately married the Princess, despite knowing how the Sea Maid felt about him.

A small coincidence can also be found in the fact that Sayaka beat herself up for wishing that she had not saved Hitomi. Wishing her friend dead, even for a moment, is practically unbearable to the justice loving, heroic Sayaka. The little Sea Maid was given a similar choice. She could prevent her own death by killing the Prince with a special dagger made by the Sea Witch. She considered this for a brief moment, and then tossed the dagger into the sea. The Sea Maid then dissolved into sea foam.[32]

32. Anderson, 91-92.

Many reviewers[33] have criticized the plot where it concerns the love triangle between Sayaka, Hitomi, and Kyosuke. They point out how it is unrealistic for Kyosuke to somehow miss the obvious fact that Sayaka, who had been showing up at the side of his hospital bed every day and bringing gifts, was in love with him. On this point, this author agrees. However, these same critics only look superficially for the explanation, calling Kyosuke Kamijo ignorant or dense.

During the early stages of research for this book, it became apparent that no image, plot element, or line of dialogue was without a purpose. *Madoka Magica* uses an extremely efficient storytelling style. There is no fluff, and no filler. Simple lines in the first two episodes which would seem to be small talk, or throwaway lines end up being surprisingly prescient foreshadowing, or deeply meaningful upon a second watch. That being the case, it would be inconsistent to spend a large portion of the dialogue of the first episode establishing the fact that Hitomi had a secret admirer, if that admirer was never to be revealed.

It may just be that the reason Kyosuke and Hitomi end up together has less to do with Sayaka's inability to make the first move than she thinks. Hitomi offered Sayaka one day to confess her feelings to Kyosuke before she did the same. Sayaka, disturbed by the realization of what she had become, and realistically filled with doubt over whether she and Kyosuke could ever have a normal relationship, did not confess her feelings to him. When Hitomi did, she and Kyosuke immediately became a couple.

The issue of who confessed first is moot. Kyosuke doesn't need words to tell him how Sayaka felt about him. Sayaka had made it abundantly clear through her actions. Let's also not forget that Hitomi was also abandoning someone who was clearly in love with her. She was giving up on her secret admirer. Unless, that is, she had found his true identity, and it was Kyosuke Kamijo all along.

---

33. Jed Blue describes Kyosuke as, "thoughtless in his behavior toward Sayaka." This is a prime example of critics not considering the possibility that Kyosuke's actions were actually deliberate. While he accepts Sayaka's gifts, he never gives any other overt indications to Sayaka that they are anything other than good friends. Blue, 33.

That would explain why Kyosuke never returned Sayaka's feelings. He was already in love with another girl. It also explains why Hitomi suddenly developed an interest in Kyosuke. She had not shown any interest in him previously. Where was she while Kyosuke was in the hospital? Nevertheless, she told Sayaka that she had liked Kyosuke for a long time and was now in love with him. It may be that her sudden change of heart was because she had finally discovered that Kyosuke was her secret love.

There are a couple of holes in this theory. Sarah Anne Williams, the voice actress who plays Sayaka, disagrees with the idea that Kyosuke could have been Hitomi's secret admirer. When asked about the idea, she expressed her opinion that Kyosuke's reaction when Hitomi confessed her love to him was too subdued for him to have been in love with her the whole time. Also, the way he neglected her in the third movie, *Rebellion*, also runs counter to the secret admirer theory. In her opinion, the real reason he does what he does is simply because, "Kyosuke's a dick!"[34]

Sarah Williams' point about Kyosuke's treatment of Hitomi is an excellent one. However, whichever interpretation of the relationship we chose, we must still ascribe an emotional disconnect to Kyosuke. Either he is not Hitomi's secret admirer, and dismisses Sayaka for no good reason, or he is Hitomi's secret admirer, and dismisses her (especially in *Rebellion*) despite having led her on with his letters. Either way, Kyosuke is somehow emotionally deficient, and at least the secret admirer theory explains the lengths to which the story goes to establish the secret admirer story element. If we do not accept Kyosuke as the admirer, then that plot thread goes nowhere, as no other explanation is ever offered. We also lose a major similarity between the Sayaka story arc and that of the *Little Sea Maid*.

Still, there are more coincidences between Sayaka and the Sea Maid. The girls' deaths are not the end of the story. Although the Anderson story would have been just fine had the

---

34. Sarah Anne Williams, personal conversation at Momocon, Atlanta, GA, 30 May 2015.

little Sea Maid dissolving into foam been the end of the tale, it continues. The Sea Maid was taken up into the spirit world, where she had a chance to earn an immortal soul by doing good deeds. In one of the more emotional scenes of *Madoka Magica*, Sayaka and Madoka watched Kyosuke perform in a concert hall, with Hitomi waiting in the wings. Madoka explained that she couldn't save Sayaka and also keep her wish intact. She asked Sayaka if she was all right with this, and Sayaka agreed, adding, "Kyosuke doesn't deserve a girl as cool as her." Madoka then asked if Sayaka was ready to go. It initially seemed like she was asking if Sayaka was ready to leave the theater, but she was really asking if Sayaka was ready to die. Sayaka agreed, and both of them faded away.(Episode 12, 15:13) It is revealed in *Rebellion* that Sayaka was actually taken up into Madoka's ascended existence to assist her as a part of the Law of Cycles. Both endings seem extraneous, yet touching, and certainly are reflections of each other.

Sisyphus and The Nutcracker

Homura Akemi is the *Nutcracker* witch. Hers, in *Rebellion*, is a strongly overt homage to the original work. While this *Nutcracker* theme is set up, at least partially, during the original series, it is not fully realized until *Rebellion*. During the original series Homura primarily plays the part of Sisyphus.[35]

Sisyphus tricked the angel of death, chained him up and returned to the world of the living. When Hades found out, he cursed Sisyphus to forever roll a rock up a hill, but the rock always slipped and fell back to the base of the hill, so Sisyphus could never complete his task. Homura went back in time, according to Gen Urobuchi, as many as a hundred times, in a vain attempt to save Madoka.[36] Most viewers believe she only repeated a single month over and over, but the story makes it clear that after she realized she could not save Madoka from becoming a witch, she (at Madoka's request) changed her tactics and began trying to

---

35. Sonnenburg, "An Opinionated Look at Madoka Magica," Episode 10.
36. Gen Urobuchi, Nitro+ Q&A Panel.

prevent Madoka from ever making a contract. Since Madoka was already a magical girl when they first met in the original timeline, Homura must have been going back farther than that in order to stop her. Thus, there is no way we can know just how long she has been trying, but one hundred months (the minimum) of trying would be more than eight years. In fact, it is probably safe to assume that Homura went back in time at least five weeks on her subsequent resets based on a statement by Madoka in episode 10 that she had been a magical girl for a week when she met Homura. That would mean Homura has been repeating time for approximately ten years. Not quite eternity, but still very reminiscent of Sysiphus' eternally unsuccessful struggle to roll the rock up the hill. Everyone (myself included) refers to Mami Tomoe as the "veteran" magical girl, but that title rightfully belongs to Homura. Compared to Homura, Mami is a rookie.

Lotte, one of Homulilly's familiars. She is clearly meant to resemble a toy soldier from *The Nutcracker*. Image source: Promotional booklet included with *Rebellion* limited edition box set.

Now let's get down to analyzing the *Nutcracker* references in Homura's story arc. First, it is important to point out that there is more than one version of the *Nutcracker*. Most people are familiar with the Tchaikovsky ballet, but that ballet was based on a book by Aleksei Dumas, who adapted his book from the original by E. T. A. Hoffman. So which version shall we compare Homura to?

The original book by Hoffman, who was German, would seem a great place to start considering Gen Urobuchi seems to have a preference for German authors. Also, Dumas' version removed many of the darker elements found in the original, and we know that Urobuchi is all about the dark stories, so that version at least can be ruled out. The problem is that the name Clara, which is the term (Clara Dolls) used for Homulilly's doll-like familiars in *Rebellion*, is only found in the ballet. In the other two versions of the *Nutcracker* story, the main character's name is Marie.

However beautiful the ballet is, it is still only a superficial representation of the original novel. Like you have heard so many times, the movie was not as good as the book. The ballet only re-creates certain scenes from the novel in music and dance, but lacks most of the specifics found in the novel. Since all the details which have found their way into *Rebellion*, with the exception of the name Clara, are found in the Hoffman novel, that is where this comparison will focus.

In E. T. A. Hoffman's novel, *The Nutcracker and the Mouse King*, Marie Stahlbaum and her brother Fritz awaited the arrival of the Christ Child to bring them gifts for Christmas. In addition to this, their godfather Drosselmeier, who was talented in the creation of clockwork animatronics, was bringing gifts for the children too. The children got exactly what they wanted for Christmas, but as usual, the most intricate items made by godfather Drosselmeier went on the top shelves of a large glass-fronted cabinet. The toys the children were allowed to play with went on the lower shelves. Fritz received toy soldiers and Marie, among other things, received a nutcracker in the shape of a man. She immediately fell in love with it.

Perhaps feeling a bit jealous, Fritz took the Nutcracker and tried to crack the largest nut he could find, which broke the Nutcracker's jaw. Marie bandaged the Nutcracker with a ribbon from her dress and stayed up late into the night with it, where she witnessed a battle between the toys, led by the Nutcracker and the mice, led by the seven headed Mouse King. All was going poorly, and the toys were losing when, just in time to save the Nutcracker from certain doom, Marie threw her shoe at the Mouse King, saving the day.

The Nutcracker, wounded in the battle, would no longer come to life. Night after night, the Mouse King came to Marie and demanded candy and other items in exchange for not killing the Nutcracker. Eventually, her brother Fritz believed her about what was going on and realized that the Nutcracker did not have a sword. He donated one from his toy soldiers and the Nutcracker once again came to life, slew the Mouse King, and took Marie off to a magical world made of candy. When she woke up, nobody believed her about what had happened. Drosselmeier then arrived with a nephew who looked suspiciously like the Nutcracker, and of course Marie fell instantly in love and they were engaged to be married.

Of course, much of the literary references in *Rebellion* are visual. This is especially true when it comes to *The Nutcracker*. Swans are a recurring image in both *The Nutcracker* and *Rebellion*. In chapter one, Marie hopes that godfather Drosselmeier had made her "a beautiful garden with a big lake, with beautiful swans swimming around wearing golden necklaces and singing pretty songs."[37] This wish comes true when, in chapter 12, the Nutcracker takes her off to his world of candy, complete with golden collared singing swans. This is triple symbolism, as a swan has its traditional symbolic association with monogamy, but in the Celtic tradition gains the symbolism of an otherworldly spirit when wearing collars or chains of precious metal[38], and again as one who is dying because swans traditionally only sing at the end of their life, thus the term 'swan song.' It is likely this symbol was chosen for *Rebellion* as a representation of Madoka, or even Homura, both of whom could be called fallen spirits or angels, but it most aptly fits Homura, who endeavors to end her own life. While swans are a visual link between the two works, they take on the added meaning of representing Homura's feelings toward Madoka, since swans are famously monogamous birds, mating for life.

How deep or intentional the visual similarities go is difficult to pin down. Interestingly, however possibly coincidentally, Marie has a doll named Gretchen, the same

---

37. E. T. A. Hoffman, *The Nutcracker and the Mouse King*, (L R C), ch. 1, accessed 27 November 2015, www.springhole.net/writing/the_nutcracker_and_the_mouse_king/.

38. Several examples of Celtic and Irish swan symbolism are found at the following sites. Silver chains: Susa Morgan Black, "The Swan," *The Order of Bards, Ovates, and Druids*, accessed 15 December 2015, http://www.druidry.org/library/animals/swan. Gold and silver chains representing descended gods: "Swan Meaning and Symbolism," *What's Your Sign*, accessed 15 December 2015, http://www.whats-your-sign.com/swan-meaning-and-symbolism.html.

Luiselotte, one of Homulilly's teeth themed familiars. Image source: Promotional booklet included with *Rebellion* limited edition box set.

name as Madoka's witch form.[39] Also, The Nutcracker's coat was vivid violet, matching the color scheme of both Homura and the toy soldier like familiars named Lotte.[40]

On a more substantial note, when Marie's brother Fritz tried to crack a nut which was too large and broke the Nutcracker's jaw, three teeth fell out. This is clearly the origin of Homura's teeth riding familiars named Louiselotte, as well as the raining teeth which can be seen in the funeral procession scene and the following battle.(*Rebellion*, 1:23:00-1:28:00) Marie tied a ribbon from her dress around the Nutcracker's broken jaw, clearly the origin of Homura's ribbon which she wears on her head.[41] All of this points to the idea that Homura broke herself trying to crack a nut which was far too big, Walpurgisnacht.[42] Years of battling the great witch to save Madoka, always ending in disaster and the death of her precious Madoka have left Homura broken, and the ribbon is a visual reminder.

Much of the imagery in *Rebellion* is drawn from chapter 4 of the Nutcracker. The arrival of the Mouse King and his army was heralded by Drosselmeier in the form of an owl perched atop a grandfather clock; a symbol seen prominently at the moment when Homura, atop the double decker bus, learned for sure that she was a witch.(*Rebellion*, 1:09:42) All of the toys and dolls which the children in *The Nutcracker* received were kept in a glass-fronted cabinet.

39. Hoffman, ch. 1.

40. Ibid, ch. 2.

41. Ibid, ch. 3.

42. In the original series' soundtrack, Walpurgisnacht's theme song is named Nux Walpurgis. Nux being Latin for nut.

After Homura learned the truth about being a witch, we saw her surrounded by items related to her witch form in a large, glass-fronted structure with many compartments. This is obviously meant to represent the cabinet from *The Nutcracker*. Marie, when confronted by the Mouse King, backed into the glass-fronted cabinet, broke it and caused a cascade of glass shards. With the glass broken, the Nutcracker and the army of toy soldiers came forth from the cabinet and did battle with the mice of the Mouse King's army. All of this is echoed when Homura, playing the part of Clara/Marie had heard enough of Kyubey's plans and held up her arm, causing the glass structure to break, and her army of dolls and toy-soldier-like familiars to attack the multitude of Kyubeys.(*Rebellion* 1:18:12) If only the bare footed Homura had a shoe to throw at Kyubey.

After the Nutcracker defeated the Mouse King, he whisked Marie off to a fantastic new world.[43] Similarly, after Homura pulled Madoka from her heavenly position, she created a utopian world and took Madoka and all her friends there. In the fantastic candy world that the Nutcracker took Marie off to, the Nutcracker displayed the power to make things happen simply by clapping his hands.[44] Likewise, in Homura's new world, she clapped her hands when she exercised her powers, like when she made Sayaka's witch form disappear.(*Rebellion*, 1:42:54)

Rebellion, like the original series, does not try to re-tell the original work in a new way, rather it takes inspiration from the source and incorporates those into an original new world. It uses the audience's familiarity with the original work to set a stage, and communicate ideas without having to resort to dialogue. It shows us characters filling familiar roles from famous works and we intuitively understand their relation to each other. When Kyubey walks up the aisle between two rows of toy soldiers toward Homura's glass fronted cabinet, we know what is about to happen.

---

43. Ibid, ch. 12.
44. Ibid, ch. 12-13.

The Mentor

Mami is problematic because her early death in the series leaves us with little story to compare to the classics. If we reduce her story arc to the basics, we get: Veteran and mentor takes on a young apprentice (in this case two: Sayaka and Madoka) and introduces that apprentice to a world of adventure and previously unknown magical powers. The veteran hints at a previous apprentice who is now estranged, and arguably evil (Kyoko).[45] This mentor is then killed by decapitation before she can train her new apprentice. The estranged, evil apprentice forms an attachment to the new apprentice (Kyoko to Sayaka), and is redeemed through self sacrifice.

These basics can be applied to many literary characters. The most striking similarity is not one from classic literature, but from classic pop culture and sci-fi. Obi Wan Kenobi was a veteran Jedi, who took on a young apprentice (Luke), hinted at an estranged apprentice (Anakin/Darth Vader) who had turned to evil, and was killed by decapitation before he could train Luke in the ways of the Jedi. In the end, Vader sacrifices himself to save Luke from the Emperor in an act of redemption which costs him his life. It could be just a coincidence, but the likeness is strong with this one.

Carrie Keranen, the voice actress who plays Mami Tomoe in the English dub of the show, also sees the similarities. When asked about the resemblance of her character's story arc to that of Obi Wan Kenobi, she said, "Oh I totally agree with this. But on a larger scale. My thought about Mami is that she is the textbook mentor character for the Hero's journey. As soon as I realized she had died, that's when I realized how important that show was. It's so

---

45. It is revealed in the *Different Story* manga that Kyoko Sakura was once Mami's apprentice, and she most certainly turned evil, allowing familiars to kill humans so they would turn into witches so she could collect the grief seeds. Masaki Hiramatsu, *Puella Magi Madoka Magica: Different Story*, illustrated by Hanokage, (Japan: Magica Quartet/Yen Press, 2014).

rare that you see a young girl go on that journey."[46]

Carrie refers to the classic "hero's journey," a commonly used, but effective storytelling device. Many of the best works of fiction follow this format, and *Star Wars* is no exception. According to Christopher Volger, a Hollywood story consultant, the basic elements of the hero's journey include: The Ordinary World, The Call to Adventure, Refusal of the Call, Meeting the Mentor, Crossing the Threshold, Tests Allies and Enemies, Approach, Ordeal, Reward, The Road Back, The Resurrection, and Return With the Elixir.[47] The names alone are fairly self explanatory, but you can see that Madoka goes through each of these as the story progresses. The first two episodes establish the ordinary world, Kyubey is a constant call to adventure, Madoka surely refuses the call, Mami is the mentor, Mami's death is where we cross the threshold (we are in the new world now, and there's no going back), Madoka then threshes out who is her ally and who is her enemy (Homura and Kyubey). In the end, the elixir which can change the world is Madoka's wish, and her transformation into the Law of Cycles. However well Mami fits in as the mentor element from the classic hero's journey, the elements such as the estranged apprentice, manner of her death, and the redemption of the former apprentice are additions to the basic format. These are elements which the Obi Wan character and Mami Tomoe have in common.

46. Carrie Keranen, email interview conducted by the author, 15 November 2015.

47. Christopher Volger, "The Hero's Journey," *Storytech Literary Consulting*, accessed 17 December 2015, http://www.thewritersjourney.com/.

The Schism or How *Rebellion* Split the Fandom

Homura splits Madoka Kaname off from the Law of Cycles. (*Rebellion*, 1:36:28)

In the first month of my *Madoka Magica* fandom experience, I was sitting in a panel at Con-Jikan, a small con put on by the University of New Mexico, at which Christine Cabanos was the guest of honor. This panel was titled, Madoka Magicanalysis: The Heroes Journey. I had just finished watching the original series, and had not seen any of the movies yet. The presenter had just finished analyzing the plot of the original series, dissecting it and explaining the elements of the classic hero's journey found within. I found this analysis fascinating and I urged him to put his presentation into book form, but unfortunately he declined. At the end of his presentation, he offered to go over some elements of *Rebellion*. This elicited a yell from the back of the room. "Homura did nothing wrong!" At that point, I knew I needed to watch the movies as soon as possible.

"Homura did nothing wrong!" has become the rallying cry for a group of fans who feel that the end of *Rebellion* was actually a fully warranted and valid ending to the movie. On the other hand, many fans fall on the opposite side of this issue, believing that Homura's actions were unjustified, and even uncharacteristic for her personality. In the interest of full disclosure, I fall firmly on the "Homura did nothing wrong!" side of the issue.

Later that week I had the opportunity to watch *Rebellion*. Just like the series, I thought I saw the ending coming, but I was wrong. I thought Madoka, acting as the Law of Cycles, would descend and take Homura's soul off to magical girl heaven in the ultimate tear jerker ending. I was prepared for that. What happened was the plot twist from hell.

The ending actually made me angry. I was worked up about it, even agitated, all day long the next day. How could Homura betray Madoka, her "very best friend" whom she loved? How could she be so selfish as to pull Madoka from the heavens, splitting the Law of Cycles, and disrespecting the wish that Madoka had made? I was convinced that the online rumors that the ending had been tacked on last minute, in order to pave the way for a sequel, were true.[48]

Eventually I calmed down, and let the critical, logical side of my brain tackle the issue. It didn't take long to realize that like most things in *Madoka Magica*, there was more to it than just the initial impression. In fact, the answer to the question, "how did Homura have the power to do that?" is the answer to all the other questions. It explains why she did it, when she decided to do it, and whether or not it was simply a horrible attempt to pave the way for an un-needed sequel.

To find the origins of this ending, we must go back to what is definitely the best episode of the original series, episode 10. We have to analyze the exact wording of Homura's wish. She didn't wish to save Madoka from Walpurgisnacht. She didn't wish to go back in time and prevent Madoka from becoming a magical girl. Homura wished to, "meet miss Kaname all over again, but this time, instead of her protecting me, I want to be strong enough to protect her!"(Original Series, episode 10, 16:40)

It was not until half way through *Rebellion* that Homura realized that she still had a wish left. That Kyubey still owed her. That Kyubey was the one she had to defeat. It came to her during the scene where she and Madoka had a conversation in a field of daises. Madoka

---

48. This excerpt from a multi-page rant on Reddit by a disgruntled fan perfectly sums up the negative reaction to the end of *Rebellion*. "So there you have it. Homura's "betrayal" of Madoka, the single most controversial event of the movie and the axis upon which possible future iterations of *Madoka Magica* will turn, was the direct result of Shinbou and Iwakami desiring franchise continuation beyond the third movie." While there is some evidence to back up this point of view, it does not, in the opinion of this author, negate the elegance and natural fit of the movie's conclusion. Novasylum, "Rebel With A Misguided Cause: How Madoka Magica Rebellion Disregards the Values of Its Own Predecessor," *Reddit*, accessed 17 December 2015, https://www.reddit.com/r/TrueAnime/comments/1wrc4k/rebel_with_a_misguided_cause_how_madoka_magica/cf4ns48.

explained that if she had a choice, she would never do anything that would take her away from Homura, her family, and the rest of her friends. Homura asked Madoka if that would be something that would hurt so much that she couldn't bear it. Homura expressed regret at failing to prevent Madoka from making her contract. It was at that moment, when the light from the airship washed over Madoka and Homura like the proverbial light bulb over an American cartoon character's head, that Homura realized what she had to do. She had to undo Madoka's wish, and defeat Kyubey so he could never again manipulate Madoka into making a contract. She must demand payment for her original wish.

There is a lot of discussion, to put it nicely, in online forums and blogs, which debate the scene where Homura actually grabs and splits Madoka. To a large extent they disagree on whether or not Homura would, or could, actually do what she did. But isn't power exactly what she wished for? She could have made any number of wishes that would have resulted in a living and happy Madoka. But she wished to be "strong enough to protect her." What gets missed in these online debates is the few scenes which follow, after Homura transforms into a demon and turns the entire universe into her labyrinth. The post credits scene shows that Kyubey is at Homura's mercy. Homura has him, and he will serve her from now on. It is also clear that she has changed his nature to allow him to feel emotion, as indicated by his look of utter, paralyzing terror.

Kyubey is defeated, but he still has his power, even if he is vulnerable. Homura, however, has more power. The entire universe is her labyrinth, and she has set the rules of this new reality. She clearly has the power to erase memories, as she explains to Sayaka when it looks like she might actually stand up to Homura. Homura even causes Sayaka's witch form to disappear with a clap of her hands. She has power; power which she can use to protect Madoka in this new, safe, predictable, gilded cage.

Whether or not this was the original ending, or one added after the original draft, is debatable. Depending how you interpret Gen Urobuchi's words, you can say that he was convinced by director Akiyuki Shinbo to change the ending from the concrete end of Homura and Madoka going off to magical girl heaven, to a more open ending, allowing the story to continue. It is probably best to allow Mr. Urobuchi to explain in his own words.

> Initially, I was planning to end this story when Homura is reunited with Madoka. There would be the classic magical girl scenes in the beginning, and then the narrative in which the secret of the town would be revealed; that would drive the beginning and middle parts, and in the end there'd be the final showdown with Kyubey.
>
> But I had a hard time deciding on the ending. Ending the story with Homura and Madoka being reunited wasn't really the best outcome. After all, the instant Homura encounters her, she'll be guided by the Law of Cycles, and disappear. Would that make her happy? It was also the director, Mr. Shinbo's opinion that the outcome of the TV series, "a human becoming a god" might be too heavy a fate for a girl in middle school to bear. Since that was the case, I decided to try to come up with a way to create a story in which Madoka could escape that outcome.
>
> But I'd already ended this story once, so it was hard to figure out how to expand it. That was when Mr. Shinbo suggested, "How about a story with Homura confronting Madoka as an enemy?" I thought, if that's at all permissible, then I'd suddenly have all these options open to me, and that's how the current plot developed.
>
> Now that I look back on it, I think it might have pushed the boundaries of the viewers' sense of morality. I'm sure there are people who view that as a "bad end," and there are probably also people who are more forgiving. I think it's an outcome that straddles that borderline. But people watch because they want to ponder whether the outcome is good or bad, so if they knew from the start that it was either a "happy end" or a "bad end", then there'd be no point in watching it in the first place. And if it's clearly a "bad end," then worse and worse things would occur, and if ten people saw it, all ten of them would be holding their heads in their hands. This film left enough room for interpretation, so it wasn't a "bad end." In that sense, I think it was the kind of film that allowed people to accept whichever outcome they liked — "happy" or "bad."
>
> Gen Urobuchi – *Rebellion* limited edition Blu-ray booklet.[49]

If you accept this explanation or not, the ending cannot simply be discounted as a shameless add-in to extend a series which had run its course. This ending, mirroring the beginning of the original series, is actually the conclusion to the loose end created by the ending of the series. Homura was the only magical girl whose wish had not been granted by the time the credits rolled in episode 12. *Rebellion* tied that lose end up nicely. This ending is a thoughtful, logical conclusion to an incredibly well written story.

But there may be a good reason why people don't feel that the ending fits well with the rest of the plot of the movie. In the beginning, Homura only seems to want to be with

---

49. Message from Gen Urobuchi in the material booklet included with the *Rebellion* limited edition Blu-ray. Accessed 18 December 2015. Translation available at: https://wiki.puella-magi.net/Rebellion_Material_Book#Message_from_Gen_Urobuchi_.28Screenplay.29.

Madoka, which is exactly what she currently has. So why does she try to solve the mystery of the labyrinth? Then she seems to have a plan to sacrifice herself to prevent Kyubey from capturing Madoka. She even yells, quite emphatically, "I have to die here!" when the rest of the magical girls try to save her. So where did this plan to try to capture Madoka come from?

In *Rebellion* there are several actions, statements, etc., where Homura seems to contradict herself. Just before capturing Madoka in the climactic scene, when Homura is seemingly most set on suicide, Madoka appears to her and tries to talk her out of it. Homura apologizes. Not for causing trouble. Not for anything she has previously done. She apologizes for committing "The worst of sins for one more chance. Even if it turned me into a monster, it wouldn't matter, as long as I could have you back."(*Rebellion*, 1:32:00) She seems to be apologizing in advance for what she is about to do: For usurping the goddess Madoka (the worst sin), becoming a demon (monster), and trapping her in a fictitious world (just so she could have her back.) There are several other scenes which indicate that her rebellion was premeditated. As previously explained, the full moon eyes with spider web tears are a symbolic representation of the plan to capture Madoka. And the "field of daisies" scene makes it clear that Homura would do anything to undo the events of the series' conclusion.

The two plans, suicide to stop Kyubey, and the usurpation of goddess Madoka, would seem to be contradictory. Unless there is more than one Homura at work, more than one plan, and they do not agree on what should be done.

Homura may be suffering from multiple personality disorder. At the very least there seem to be three distinct personalities at work, with their own goals and desires. These three personalities seem to be represented visually by costume changes. The innocent, perhaps even happy, glasses-Homura (sometimes called Moemura by fans) is represented by the pigtails and glasses which she wears at the beginning of the movie. This personality is fairly content, only wants to be with Madoka, and is her original personality. Normal Homura is visually represented by straight hair, no glasses, and black tights, all of which she wore in the original series. This Homura is the confident, decisive, but damaged Homura from the majority of the original series. She wants to solve the mystery of who created the labyrinth which is their world in the *Rebellion* movie, and she will do anything to protect Madoka. Finally we have Homura Akuma, or demon/devil Homura. She only fully appears at the very end of the movie, but her influence can be felt during certain scenes, particularly the "field of daisies" and the "Mouse King vs. the Nutcracker" scenes. She is visually represented by the Homura who appears identical to normal Homura, but watch for the red hair ribbon. This ribbon is not worn by regular Homura, only by the warped, selfish personality who wants to change the game, defeat Kyubey, and usurp, capture, and keep Madoka for herself. She is selfish, powerful, and dangerous.

As the movie progresses, glasses-Homura disappears, replaced by the true Homura, who is in turn replaced by Homura Akuma until the final scene where she sprouts her black raven wings, becomes the dominant personality, and assumes total control. It is also important to note that this ribbon-Homura also had wings during the last scenes of the original series.

Often Homura will visually transform on screen. Sometimes it is as simple as unbraiding her hair and taking off her glasses. Other times she changes instantaneously. In at least one instance, Madoka unsuccessfully attempts to transform normal Homura back into glasses-Homura by re-braiding her hair. These changes in appearance would seem to be a visual signal to the viewer, meant to indicate which personality is currently dominant.

Example of transformation: (*Rebellion*, 1:21:48)

The above three images were taken from the "twin chairs" scene, where Homura and Madoka sit in a grassy field in two identical white chairs, right next to each other. This theme is repeated throughout the movies, and the promotional materials for the movies. But here, Madoka stands on her chair, stretches out her arms like one who is nailed to a cross, falls from her chair and splatters on the ground. Glasses-Homura jumps up to save her, and in mid stride she sheds her moe exterior, becoming the Homura Akemi who is dedicated to saving Madoka. This is a metaphor for the events of the original series, where Homura's efforts to save Madoka forged her into the strong and powerful character that she became. Also, just as in the original series, she is unable to stop Madoka from sacrificing herself, and the metaphor continues, with her smashing herself with her own fist as an expression of her own self-hate. She cannot forgive herself for allowing Madoka to sacrifice herself.

But is the emergence of Devil Homura a result of Homura's guilt or self-loathing? Has she subconsciously decided that her former self is unworthy of Madoka, and created a new, powerful personality capable of doing the things which her weaker self could never do? Or could this final personality be an unavoidable fate set in motion in the original series? Could this simply be the answer to her original wish? At the end of the original series, Homura was the only magical girl whose wish had not been granted. Homura didn't save Madoka. Madoka saved herself, seemingly making Homura's wish irrelevant. The series ends, with Homura's contract still unpaid.

The end of *Rebellion* sees Homura's contract finally paid in full. After she pulls ultimate Madoka from heaven, she re-orders the universe so that Kyubey is no longer a threat to Madoka. Then we see her presiding over the other magical girls as they walk to school.

Madoka and Homura have switched places, physically and metaphorically. Homura is now the local girl, and Madoka is the transfer student. They re-do their first meeting, but this time, instead of Madoka protecting Homura, Homura has seemingly unlimited power. The dangerous and powerful Devil Homura may actually be the answer to her own original wish.

But this theme is still further entwined with the original series, because that wish may also explain why Homura was never able to defeat Walpurgisnacht. Walpurgisnacht was the clockwork witch, and Homura Akemi was the magical girl of time. So why, after an unlimited number of tries, should she fail to defeat a witch that operates on the same (seemingly) theme as her own powers? Simple. Homura never wished to defeat Walpurgisnacht. She wished to have the power to protect Madoka. Walpurgisnacht was never the true threat to Madoka. Even if Homura had destroyed Walpurgisnacht, another witch would have come along to take her place. Madoka would never be safe. Kyubey wanted to turn Madoka into a witch and harness her energy, which would thereby destroy humanity, and Madoka. Homura's wish empowered her to protect Madoka from her true enemy, Kyubey. A wish granted by the very creature it would damn. In the end of *Rebellion*, Homura's wish is granted to perfection. Kyubey is defeated, there is no more threat to Madoka, and Homura even gets to re-do her initial meeting with Madoka. The perfect wish, interpreted imperfectly by the wish maker.

Homura, and the audience, both interpreted that the wish empowered Homura to save Madoka from that which killed her. But Homura's wish enabled her to defeat Kyubey, not Walpurgisnacht. Her wish empowered her not to protect Madoka's body, an item reduced to a tool by this anime, but to protect that which truly mattered, her soul. Defeating Kyubey saved Madoka, and every other magical girl that is or ever will be.

In the closing scenes of *Rebellion*, Kyoko is seen wasting food, tossing apples to Homura's raven familiars and into the drainage ditch/stream which carries them away. It is both a clue to the fact that this is not the world we are familiar with, but more importantly, it is evidence that Kyoko no longer suffers from the psychological scars which caused her to revile the wasting of food. In other words, Kyoko no longer remembers the trauma of her past. All has been healed. Madoka is not the only magical girl saved by Homura's transgression. The world is truly a better place. Much as Madoka saved the souls of the magical girls, Homura has erased that which caused their despair. From the beginning, Homura has been the one to suffer, immeasurably, for others. In the end, Homura is the one who has set the world to rights. If any character in this story is the hero, or heroine, it is her.

The end of *Rebellion* was certainly not tacked on just to keep the franchise going. Although that may have been an intentional effect of this ending, the ending was not an afterthought. It is a poetic, well thought out, balanced ending which closes all the holes and ties up all the loose ends of the original series. More importantly, it is fully in keeping with the character of Homura. This researcher fully believes that she was justified in what she did, that it was something that she would have chosen to do, and that Homura did nothing wrong.

-...Will Rebellion be the end of the story for the five magical girls?

Shinbo: Madoka isn't a story where everyone comes out with the same feelings. I think different people will draw different conclusions about the ending. How they accept it will be up to the viewers themselves.[50]

Interview with Akiyuki Shinbo and Gen Urobuchi in New Type 2013-09

Next we will likely see the Combat of the Angels, as hinted about in *Eternal*. The war in heaven is coming, with the magical girls playing the roles of the angels, Madoka in the role of God, and Homura reprising her role as Lucifer. Which angels will flock to which banner? Will Mami fight Homura to rescue her old master, Kyubey? Those two never really got along anyway. Will Kyoko join Homura against Mami? That would pit her against Sayaka; an almost unthinkable situation for her. But she was always a pragmatic girl, Kyubey must be stopped, and Homura's solution accomplishes that. One thing is for sure, Sayaka will not forsake Madoka. And in the end, can Homura ever really harm Madoka? This battle seems fated to end just like its biblical inspiration.

In the final scenes of *Rebellion*, Homura deliberately breaks a teacup. This is a chilling bit of foreshadowing which indicates that she intends to harm or even kill Mami Tomoe, whose death in the original series was also symbolized with a broken teacup. The author recently had the distinct pleasure of asking Carrie Keranen if she believes Mami can stand up to Homura now. So far, Mami has an undefeated record against Homura, but now that Homura is the author of the new universe, things have changed. Carrie said, "I think in this realm Homura is now even more powerful than any of us can imagine and it is impossible to know what she would do in order to keep Madoka trapped in her menagerie. Even the last battle I didn't technically win.... Homura chose to shoot me in the leg. I think that the part of her that allowed that bit of conscience in that moment is now gone and she would stop at nothing to

50. This excerpt from an interview in *New Type* magazine was conducted before the release of *Rebellion*. It is clear that director Akiyuki Shinbo was concerned about the fan reaction to the ending. Interview with Akiyuki Shinbo and Gen Urobuchi, *New Type* 2013-09, accessed 6 December 2015, http://wiki.puella-magi.net/NewType_2013-09.

remain at the top. Only Madoka has any chance of defeating Homura. The best Mami can do is to help Madoka remember who she truly is inside. It's their only chance. Even Kyubey was frightened of Homura."[51]

Do we even need another sequel? Tristan "Arkada" Gallant says emphatically, "The Madoka Magica series did not need a sequel, but this film, this film right here, certainly does!"[52] I would have to agree with Arkada, this story is not complete, and there have been too many bits of foreshadowing which hint at a continuation. However, if we look at the money, that is probably the best indicator of future installments. *Madoka Magica the Movie: Rebellion* earned 1.9 billion yen at the box office in Japan when it came out in 2013, breaking a record previously held by *K-ON!*[53] Studios rarely let a series with record breaking profits sit for long. Money talks, and it's screaming, "More Madoka!"

To be honest, I don't know if it would be a good idea to add more to this story. Messing with perfection is normally a recipe for disaster, and that is exactly how I felt when I first heard about *Rebellion*. But *Rebellion* proved me wrong. Very few intellectual properties have been able to maintain their quality when producing a sequel to a sequel. Let's just hope that the next installment of *Madoka Magica* is more along the lines of *The Last Crusade* than *The Kingdom of the Crystal Skull*.

51. Carrie Keranen, email interview.

52. Tristan "Arkada" Gallant, "Glass Reflection Review of Madoka Magica the Movie: Rebellion," *Youtube*, accessed 17 October 2015, https://www.youtube.com/watch?v=PujoJKtqHSU.

53. Ejc, "3rd Madoka Magica Film Tops K-ON! Film's Box Office," *Anime News Network*, accessed 17 October 2015, http://www.animenewsnetwork.com/news/2013-12-22/3rd-madoka-magica-film-tops-k-on-film-box-office.

SYMBOLOGY

Homura's witch form, Homulilly, surrounded by symbols representing her nature as a time traveler. (*Rebellion*, 1:22:02)

Madoka Magica is a story filled with symbolism and metaphor. The original series had many visual symbols, but not nearly as many as *Rebellion*. The witch labyrinths had symbols which gave clues to the nature of the magical girl from whom the witch was born. Homura Akemi's home featured a giant swinging pendulum, and furniture arranged in the shape of a clock face, symbolic of her time travelling ability. There were Christian and other religious symbols used throughout the series, but the story was mostly told through the action and dialogue. In *Rebellion*, however, symbols become as important as the dialogue to the telling of the story. Few movies ever reach the level of visual density displayed in *Rebellion*. To explain or theorize on all of the symbols in *Rebellion* could be a life's work. Akiyuki Shinbo and Gekidan Inu Curry have taken symbolism to a new height with this movie.

Yet some critics, such as *Youtube* anime reviewer Kevin Nyaa,[54] have claimed that the ubiquitous symbols were thrown in just to up the visual density, and make the viewer assume a deeper meaning than there really is. Is that the case, or do all these symbols really have meaning? This chapter will explore both sides of that coin.

(Rebellion, 1:23:02)

Clearly the majority of symbols in this movie are meaningful. The image which starts off the chapter is a prime example. Homulilly is Homura Akemi's witch form. She has a witches hat which is deformed into a stylized phonograph, complete with record (the hat's brim) and needle (the point of the hat). This is an obvious reference to the events of the original series, where she unsuccessfully tried again and again to turn back time and save Madoka. Her life has been a broken record, repeating as many as a hundred times. Next to her is a giant spinning circle with the silhouette of an hourglass, and runes which translate into phrases such as "resignation," "passion," and "sad memories." Across the face of this wheel of time is the silhouette of the same pendulum which swung in her home back in the real world. And the far background is made up of the gears of an analog clock; all symbols of her repeating time, failure to save Madoka, and the despair caused by her failure.

Then there are other images, such as the one shown to the right of this page, which seem to have random symbols thrown in just to fill the space.

Madoka's transformation sequence. *(Rebellion:* 0:19:50)

54. Kevin Nyaa, "The Problems With: Madoka Magica Rebellion."

Madoka surrounded by the symbols of the other magical girls. *Key Animation Note, vol 6*.

Admittedly, if the space were not filled with these seemingly random symbols, it would be a stark contrast to the visual density of the rest of the film, and so this space would cry out to be filled with something. Compare that image to the one on the left side of this page, and you will find distinct similarities, but the symbols are different. If you look closely, you will see that both images contain four pointed stars or diamonds (a symbol associated with Homura) and flowers (a symbol associated with Mami), but the clover, key and keyhole are unique to the first image, and do not seem to fit with any symbols commonly associated with the other magical girls. The katakana in the previous image simply spells Madoka, not very deep or overly thoughtful on the part of the artist. One could look at the heart shaped handle on the key and say that it resembles the heart shaped cutout on the back of Madoka's magical girl costume. The keyhole would seem to represent a character closely related to the one for whom the key stands. But are we now doing exactly as critic Kevin Nyaa suggests, and ascribing meaning to images which were simply thrown in to fill the space? No. In fact, all the answers

The same key from Madoka's transformation sequence, in a glass jar. (*Rebellion*, 1:10:29)

are contained within the movie if one is willing to put in the effort to search for them.

Hitomi Shizuki, the green haired girl is fittingly represented by the clover. She wears slippers with clovers on them, and the clover is prominently displayed over the scene where her nightmare is subdued by the magical girls. The key with a heart shaped handle is also a

The clover, with a bird superimposed, likely symbolizing how Homura influences Hitomi's nightmare. Close inspection reveals clovers in the backs of the chairs as well.(*Rebellion*, 0:03:21)

recurring image in *Rebellion*. It's most meaningful use is during the scene where Homura realizes that she is the witch in whose labyrinth all of the girls are trapped. In that scene, the world begins to burn (fire being another symbol for Homura's despair) and for an instant we catch a glimpse of this very key, inside a glass jar. This is very likely a visual metaphor for how Homura has trapped Madoka inside a (now) fragile container, her labyrinth.

How can we know for sure the key represents Madoka? We can't, but let's take a closer look at the key as a symbol. Inside the heart shaped cutout of the smaller key is a tear drop, the shape of Madoka's soul gem. Not only that, but this is a specific type of key. This key is the type used to open the case of a grandfather clock. Also, this is not the only form the key takes. Other times the key appears with an exaggerated, wide handle. This is a distinct type of key, one used to wind a grandfather clock. This relationship is such that the key is the source of the clock's power, as Madoka is the source of Homura's strength and determination. One could certainly make a case that the keys refer to Homura, but both keys, despite being associated with time, also have attributes which seem to indicate Madoka, and that is the interpretation which I have adopted for the purpose of this book. So, to answer Mr. Nyaa, the symbols in the background are not random filler, lazily thrown in to imply more meaning than the artist truly intended. There is a pattern, and that pattern can, despite Jed Blue's insistence to the contrary, be deciphered.[55]

Grandfather clock key with hourglass symbol on the handle. Image source: Howard Miller USA, accessed 15 July 2015, http://www.howardmillerusa.com/parts-and-accessories.html

55. Blue, 104.

It's tempting to try to find a deep meaning to every shape that pops onto the screen, but even if we accept that every symbol was thoughtfully placed there, it would be a tedious effort to catalogue them all, and hold little entertainment value to review them. For these reasons, this chapter will stick to the larger and obviously intentional symbols which add to the appreciation of the story.

Closeup of key in the symbol-churn which appears just before Homura's meeting with Kyoko. (*Rebellion*, 0:30:23).

The challenge in exploring the symbolism in *Rebellion* is the sheer volume of it. It may seem logical to go chronologically, beginning with the opening scene, explaining such things as the successive windows which the camera flies through when the girls enter the room to confront Hitomi's nightmare for the first time. Each window has symbols corresponding to the five girls, a witch, or to Bebe/Charlotte. One opens to a black screen with yellow flower silhouettes, followed by a deer with a fork in it.

Grandfather clock winding key. Image source: Grand father Clocks Plus, accessed 15 July 2015, http://www.grandfatherclocksplus.com/cgi-bin/shop/DoorKey.html.

I bring this one up specifically because it is the one image which really catches the eye as this fast paced series of imagery flies by. It's clear that the flowers are a representation of Mami, as the symbol on her soul gem is flower shaped, but if you are paying attention you will also notice that the deer is associated with her. We can see the heads of deer mounted as trophies on things which are associated with Mami, such as her fruit parfait shaped, railroad mounted, nuke cannon which she fires at the giant Lockes during the battle with Homulilly. The fork is a recurring image also. It has been associated with the sweets witch, Charlotte, since the original series. That same sweets witch makes multiple insinuations that she wants to eat Mami during the *Rebellion* movie. A deer with a fork in it

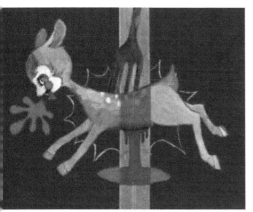
Deer impaled with a fork. (*Rebellion*, 0:03:15)

seems an apt metaphor for such an element, which recalls the events of the infamous third episode.

That is just one of the several windows in this scene, which lasts only seconds. As you can see, to go chronologically through each of *Rebellion's* bursts of imagery would fill hundreds, maybe thousands of pages. Rather than that, this chapter will select only the images which are recurring, such as the swan or the moon, and imagery which only comes up once but is central to the point being communicated, such as when the spider lilies atop Homulilly's head suddenly transform into cherry blossoms. In other words, this chapter will translate those images which are central to the plot, and teach you the basics of the symbolic language, so that you can gain a better appreciation for that part of the story communicated through symbolism and metaphor. It is this author's hope that you will translate those images for yourself while watching the show, which is of course the most enjoyable way to read them.

First, it is useful to start with the basics. The following symbols are associated with the five main characters, and are used in both the original series, and heavily in the *Rebellion* movie.

Homura Akemi

Homura Akemi has the greatest number of symbols associated with her. She is most closely associated with clocks, gears, and pendulums. Like all of the girls, the shape of her soul gem is regularly used in imagery related to her. The gem is in the shape of a diamond, or four pointed star. This is very likely a reference to her power over time, since "diamonds are forever." In *Rebellion*, anything nutcracker or toy soldier related is hers. In that same line are images of mouths, teeth, etc. The scene of her biting her own soul gem is a powerful *Nutcracker* reference. Her name, which Madoka aptly points out means flame, gives us another symbol which is regularly used in connection to her, especially in association with her despair. The salamander is often seen in association with Homura, and seems an odd fit at first. However, in the Middle Ages, the salamander was associated with fire. This is possibly due to the salamander living inside rotten logs. When these logs were thrown onto a fire, the salamanders would run out of the fire, leading the medieval witnesses to believe that they lived in, or were born of the fire.[56]

The *Rebellion* movie also brings another new symbol, the swan, to symbolize Homura's devotion to Madoka. Other birds are also seen in association with Homura. They can be seen as very small details, such as in the wrought iron of the bus stop where she gets on the double decker bus to separate herself from her soul gem, or inside the clocks which fill the seats of that bus. Birds are also one of the forms of her witch familiars, taking the form of diamond eyed ravens. This is perhaps a reference to the Native American trickster god who created the world, since Homura created the labyrinth which is effectively their world and simultaneously a deception.

Ultimate Madoka's witch form. (Episode 12, 08:44)

As discussed earlier, the red spider lily is a symbol associated with death, and as such is used often to symbolize Homura's desire to die in order to protect Madoka. When Madoka reaches into Homura's labyrinth through an open window to convince her not to take her own life, her salvation is visually represented when her red spider lilies, the symbol of death, are replaced by cherry blossoms, a symbol for a short but beautiful life.

Madoka

Madoka has remarkably few symbols associated with her for being the title character. Anything pink is probably a reference to her, but specific examples are often ribbons, threads,

---

56. Malcolm Gill, "Research Letter 22, SALAMANDERS as SYMBOLS," *Firebreak*, accessed 15 January 2016, http://www.firebreak.com.au/resletter22.html.

flowers (especially roses), and hearts. In *Rebellion*, the symbol most strongly associated with Madoka is the moon, because her witch form incorporated this imagery. The key can be associated with Madoka, and the key hole with Homura. They are so closely related as to be difficult to tell which represents which, but it would seem, especially considering the specific shape of the key in the symbol-churn depicted on page 57, that this assessment is the correct one. Anyone who has wound a true grandfather clock knows the unusual shape of that crank. It is a wide handled key, which fits into a keyhole on the clock face. In the framework of symbols in *Madoka Magica*, the clock is always associated with Homura, so it is logical that the winding key which keeps that clock running would be Madoka.

Sayaka

Sayaka is often associated with water, or the color blue. Her soul gem is reminiscent of a pearl in an oyster, but is also a runic musical note. Musical notes, clefs, instruments, or concert halls are also associated with her. The image of the valiant, sword wielding knight is also hers. The mermaid is of course her best known symbol, but her armor-clad, half-mermaid, half orchestra conductor witch form also uses wheels as weapons. These wheels are sometimes used as a symbol for Sayaka or her witch form Oktavia, and are probably a reference to the train on which she lost her faith in humanity, abandoned her commitment to protecting people and (it is implied that she) killed two men. Musical imagery is strongly associated with her, and a great example can be seen on the walls of the intersection where she talks to Homura after her epic gun battle with Mami. These instrument covered walls, and water covered streets let us know who is really in control at this point. Sayaka has all the information, all the answers which Homura has been seeking, and she is not inclined to give it up. Homura by contrast is lost and confused, and Sayaka even prevents her from using her time manipulation ability. This scene clearly belongs to Sayaka.

Kyoko

Kyoko's soul gem, as well as elements of her magical girl costume, evoke the symbol of an eye. Notice how her soul gem hangs on her chest in the middle of an oval shaped cutout in her costume, and the white lines which are drawn vertically on her boots also form an eye at the top front of her boot cuffs. Her soul gem fits into her hair pin, which has a convenient circular cutout which again makes it into an eye.

Her witch form, Ophelia, not seen on screen during the series or any of the movies, but seen in supplemental material, rides a horse and has a candle for a head. The candle and the horse may be used as symbols for Kyoko on rare occasions. However, do not get confused, as the horse is also a symbol for the witch Elly, whose labyrinth featured carousel horses. After that, the apple is the symbol most commonly associated with Kyoko, but it is usually used to represent the sins of her past, rather than a symbol for her as a character.

Kyoko's soul gem hangs in the middle of the cutout on her chest, creating the semblance of an eye. (*Beginnings*, 1:18:08)

Mami

Mami has perhaps the least number of symbols associated with her. Obviously her soul gem's flower shape is regularly used. Specifically, the flower is a daisy. Carrie Keranen pointed out the importance of the daisy as a symbol. When asked why she believed Mami's symbol was a flower, she said, "Honestly, I am not sure, but it seems like a daisy to me, and the symbology works." She pointed out how the Latin, or scientific name for the daisy is Bellis Perennis. The word bellis could be derived from bello, the Latin word for war. She also pointed out how the daisy is also associated with healing. "That ability to heal wounds and the fact that its name may come from "war." It stands for resilience and childhood and let's face it, the way she became a magical girl fits that to a "T.""[57]

Other than the daisy, she is usually represented by the mounted heads of deer, probably a reference to her use of rifles, a hunter's weapon. There are two skeletal deer heads mounted

---

57. Carrie Keranen, email interview.

outside her home in *Rebellion*, and her train-mounted railroad gun has two deer heads on it. In *Rebellion*, Mami is sometimes referred to as cheese, based on her yellow costume, soul gem, and hair, as well as the fact that Charlotte ate her in the original series. Charlotte, in the form of Bebe or Nagisa, often makes references to Mami turning into cheese, and her desire to eat that cheese.

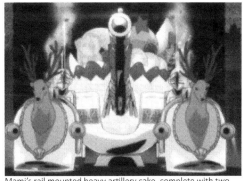

Mami's rail mounted heavy artillery cake, complete with two trophy mounted deer. (*Rebellion*, 1:30:12)

The Sweets Witch

Charlotte, Bebe, or Nagisa has a surprising number of symbols associated with her for having only had a short appearance in the original series. Having been the sweets witch, cake or dessert foods are of course a symbol for her. Her very head evokes the shape of a candy wrapper. Additionally, the fork is also associated with her. Before Nagisa's official character design was made public, fans depicted her in art as using a fork and knife as her magical girl weapons. This fork, although no longer her weapon, continues to be used as a symbol in *Rebellion* and can be seen during one of the first scenes involving Homura's Clara Doll familiars, who turn a hand crank attached to a gear which churns a mixture of symbols including a strawberry, fork, horse, moon, scissors, wheel, key and a quickly sinking cog wheel. These aren't just symbols for the girls, but symbols associated with the witches of the series, including Gertrud's scissors. Atop this collection of symbols is the salamander, giving the audience a spoiler, if they can read the symbols, as to who is responsible for creating this world.

The symbol-churn, the handle is turned by one of Homura's familiars while her own salamander icon rests on top. (*Rebellion*, 0:30:23)

Apples

Kyoko Sakura has an eating disorder. When her family was destitute and they didn't know where their next meal would come from, it affected her deeply. Once she came into her powers, and was forced to take care of herself as an orphan, she hoarded food, was constantly eating, and became violent whenever she witnessed food being wasted.

Kyoko feeds apples to Homura's familiars. (*Rebellion*, 1:41:32)

Even this eating disorder was used as a symbol to communicate meaningful ideas within the story. When Kyoko attempts to befriend any other character, she does so by offering them food. Considering how important food is to her, offering it to anyone is a very significant gesture. When she brings Sayaka to her father's old church, and explains how she became a magical girl, she offers Sayaka a peace offering in the form of an apple. Sayaka, although sympathetic to Kyoko's plight, sees her flaws and wants nothing to do with her. She rejects the apple, the symbol of Kyoko's past sins, and her offer of friendship.

As stated earlier, in the Christian tradition, apples are used to represent original sin. Sayaka's rejection of the apple can be interpreted as a rejection of Kyoko's violent and selfish past, and tossing it away is a way of saying that she will not make the same mistakes that Kyoko did. It is also interesting to note that in the final scenes of *Rebellion*, Kyoko is seen wasting food, offering apples to the birds before throwing them into the water. It would seem that Homura's re-writing of the universe has erased the sin which led to Kyoko's suffering. At the very least she no longer remembers, and no longer suffers from the traumatic events of her past which led to her eating disorder.

Cheese

Charlotte was the sweets witch. Her labyrinth was filled with candy, cakes, pies, etc. There was no cheese in it. Why then is Bebe obsessed with cheese? The answer is in the Cake Song. Each of the girls identifies themselves with a food, and all but one is a fruit. Mami is the cheese. When Bebe wants her to transform into her magical girl form, she says, "Turn into cheese!" Mami's hair, magical girl costume, and eyes are all yellow, and in episode three, Charlotte eats her. Not just her head, she feasts gleefully on her body as well. When the girls are explaining why they came to save Homura at the end of *Rebellion*, Nagisa/Bebe says that she just wanted one more chance to eat cheese again. This comparison of Mami to cheese makes the Cake Song scene especially creepy, adding a subtle sense that something is wrong, despite the happiness of all the girls in the scene. Considering her attachment to cheese, it is worth noting that Nagisa's transformation involves the filling of a Nagisa-shaped glass vessel with milk.

The Moon

This is a symbol which is used in *Rebellion* to represent ultimate Madoka. This comes from the final scenes of the end of the original series, or of the second movie, *Eternal*. After ascending, Madoka explains to Homura that because of the way she phrased her wish, she doesn't have to worry about transforming into a witch. Madoka fires her bow and defeats her own witch form, just before it can destroy the world. In this scene we see that ultimate Madoka's witch takes the form of a moon, half of its face black in shadow, and the other half lit.

In *Rebellion* we see this form repeated, sometimes as foreshadowing, such as when we are shown a close up of Homura's face where she is crying spider web tears, and her eyes have been replaced by pink moons. In the post credit scene, we see Homura dancing and frolicking under an unusual half-moon. Unusual in that it is not just in shadow, but only half present. We know this because we can see stars where the other half of this moon should be. The moon is only half present because Homura has split Madoka in two, separating the individual girl from the larger concept of the Law of Cycles.

Ribbons

Ribbons have multiple meanings in *Madoka Magica*. Obviously, Mami uses ribbons as her primary power, using them to cut like blades, as restraints to trap an opponent, wrapping them around Homura's leg to negate her time stop ability, and shaping them into rifles and decoys. But when used for symbolic effect, they are usually associated with Madoka. Their association with Madoka is obvious, as they are given to her in the opening scenes of *Beginnings*. However, she gives these ribbons to Homura after she ascends; a memento to help Homura remember her. This is the beginning of the *Nutcracker* references which will pervade the *Rebellion* story. Like the Nutcracker, who wears Clara's ribbon on its head to mend its broken jaw, Homura wears Madoka's ribbon on her head. This is a strong reminder that Homura is incomplete without Madoka, and that the events of the last decade (that's right, decade) of watching her best friend die over and over again were too much for her, and she has serious mental and emotional scars.

The ribbon ties in to Homura's original wish. Cristina Vee gives the following interpretation of the motive behind that wish: "Homura felt like she had a debt to repay to Madoka. She didn't want to feel defenseless anymore, she wanted to be [on the] front line with her. I also think that she wanted to be Madoka's white knight."[58] At the end of the original series, Madoka gave Homura the ribbon, like a medieval lady handing her token or favor to the knight in shining armor who fights for her honor. In the end of *Rebellion*, Homura feels like she is no longer in Madoka's service, and returns the ribbon, rejecting her role as Madoka's knight.

The ribbon also represents an emotional bond between her and Madoka. The *Puella Magi Wiki* page has a detailed explanation of the yuri undertones present in *Madoka Magica*, which honestly does a better job explaining this theme than I could. That webpage is primarily filled with fan speculation and opinion, but nevertheless contains a useful description of how the red ribbon may be a symbol borrowed from another magical girl anime, *Magical Girl Lyrical Nanoha*, where the characters Nanoha and Fate exchange red ribbons, and also refer to each other as best friends, much like Homura and Madoka.[59] The best evidence for the connection is that both shows, *Madoka Magica* and *Lyrical Nanoha* share the same director, Akiyuki Shinbo. In this case, the red ribbon may be a representation of the red string of fate. Another example of this red string of fate, the recurring image of pink string on a spool, is kicked by Homura's familiars, seemingly as a metaphor to represent Homura's rejection of Madoka's sacrifice. (*Rebellion*, 1:11:58) This red string is the Chinese equivalent of our western idea of a soul mate, binding two people who are destined to be together.

58. Cristina Vee, email correspondence with the author, 29 June 2016.

59. "Yuri Undertones," *Puella Magi Wiki*, accessed 29 December 2015, https://wiki.puella-magi.net/Yuri_undertones.

Later, when Homura is verbally confronting Kyubey before their final showdown, she is surrounded by the same red yarn which appears in Hitomi's nightmares. Here the yarn indicates the connection between Homura and Hitomi, and this one is not a happy connection. It is possible that Hitomi's nightmare is entirely controlled (subconsciously?) by Homura.

Windows

Windows appear in the majority of witch labyrinths from the original series, including Charlotte's. The window, in its most basic form, is a portal to the outside world. In *Rebellion* it is a portal through which Madoka reaches into Homura's labyrinth to save her from herself. It may even be the representation of the entrance through which the witch's victims are allowed inside. Still, the presence of a window implies a wall, or a barrier. It separates the inside world from the outside, and it signifies to the viewer that we are inside the labyrinth. When Homura and Kyoko attempt to take the bus to Kazamino city, it repeatedly passes the Kazamino stop, bringing them back to Mitakihara. A keen eye can spot that Kazamino Station (visible briefly as they speed by) is entirely composed of thousands of windows, a symbol for the entry/exit of Homura's labyrinth.

The window is also the great spoiler of *Rebellion*. It is actually present in the first few seconds of the movie, floating behind Homura's soul gem during the opening monologue, indicating not just that this story takes place in a labyrinth, but even whose labyrinth it is. Just like in the original series, where Madoka's friends try to explain how she could have seen Homura in her dream before she had ever met her, this is an example of a huge spoiler hidden in plain sight. It is hidden only because it does not make sense out of context, but after having seen the entire show, you realize that you were given the basics of the plot at the beginning, but didn't realize it at the time.

Ultimate Madoka reaches through a window to comfort the suicidal Homura. Literally a helping hand from outside the labyrinth. (*Rebellion*, 1:31:48)

On that note, the opening credit

sequence is just as much of a spoiler. A hand with a white bracelet turns a desert into a garden. Kyubey's tower, where Homura is imprisoned appears briefly in the background until that same hand transforms the desolate landscape into a lake. Then we see all the girls dancing around a clearly unhappy Homura. But the big giveaway comes when we see Homura behind a giant cog wheel, clothed in a white dress, and wearing white bracelets. It was Homura's hands which were creating the idealized world in which the other girls were happily dancing.

The Hands

The theme of hands continues, although they are no longer wearing the white bracelets. They are seen in both of the nightmares which the girls battle (both of which are Hitomi's). They don't really seem to be doing anything, they just float next to the stuffed animal creature which represents Hitomi's nightmare.

They can be seen on other occasions too, if you are paying attention. They are seen depositing Homura's familiars into the city later in the movie, and constructing the city itself during the scene where Kyubey explains how he has used Homura as bait for the Law of Cycles. Hitomi's nightmare has a tag which reads "Made in Cabinet" on one side, and "Homulilly" on the other, indicating a connection to Homura. The cabinet is the glass-fronted one from *The Nutcracker*.

During Homura's transformation sequence before the battle with the nightmare, the words "To Master: We are bored" appear written in runes, possibly indicating that Homura is conjuring the nightmares to keep either her friends, or her familiars distracted or entertained.

The Unicorn

Even though this symbol only appears once, it is worth mentioning because of its prominence. When Kyoko tries to enlist Madoka's help to rescue Sayaka, they speak in the street, framed by two wind chimes. The one on the left is a mermaid, which obviously represents Sayaka, the object of the conversation and the objective of their mission. On the right side is a unicorn. Even without considering the nature of unicorns, it seems somehow appropriate that it should represent Kyoko. It is a beautiful piece of foreshadowing, depicting the upcoming scene where Kyoko battles the witch Oktavia. The unicorn's horn seems an appropriate representation of Kyoko's spear, pointed at her adversary, the mermaid witch.

However, the unicorn has an appropriate symbolic meaning here. Although it is a symbol found in many cultures around the world, it is a powerful Christian symbol, appearing at least eight times in the Bible. It was also commonly used in the middle ages as a symbol for Christ.[60] This makes it a most appropriate symbol for representing Kyoko, the daughter of a Christian minister. On top of this, the unicorn's horn was reputed to have the power to "purify polluted or poisonous waters."[61] The unicorn and the mermaid wind chimes aptly represent Kyoko, the Christian magical girl attempting to restore the soul of Sayaka, the magical girl of water.

Kyoko and Madoka talk in the street, framed by a symbolic representation of the upcoming battle. (Episode 9, 12:44)

Rebellion is a movie made specifically for those who are highly familiar with the original series. I can only imagine how confusing it must be for those who go in cold, without having seen the series or the two recap movies. At a minimum it demands that you at least know the events of the series in order to grasp the differences, which are subtle but give the viewer that feeling that something is off. If you don't have the original series to compare the opening act of *Rebellion* to, you will miss the suspense which it is intended to build. However, that is only the minimum familiarity needed to comprehend the message. The original series inspired

60. Margaret Starbird, "Unicorns," Sacred Union in Christianity, accessed 17 December 2015, http://www.marga retstarbird.net/unicorn.html.

61. Ibid.

many fans to actually pick the details apart. Fans with this level of knowledge are rewarded with Easter egg foreshadowing. If you know what you are looking at, you will realize very early in the movie, perhaps before the credits roll, that the entire movie takes place in a witch labyrinth. As pointed out above, the window appears in nearly every single witch labyrinth. But the movie is filled with other images which are plucked from those labyrinths; scissors from Gertrud's labyrinth, carousel horses from Elly's labyrinth, tall legged tables and chairs from Charlotte's labyrinth, etc. Homura's gondola scene is a prime example. She has already begun to suspect that she is the witch, but to drive that point home she rides in a gondola which is shaped like a horse right out of Elly's labyrinth. The pole in the middle of the gondola is not a mast; it is the pole which attaches the horse to the carousel.

Armed with the above information, watching the *Rebellion* movie should be a different experience. Unlike the original series, the entire *Rebellion* movie takes place in Homura's witch labyrinth, which allowed director Akiyuki Shinbo to leverage the creative genius of Inu Curry's designs to craft a visual experience without the restraints of having to depict the real world. Much of Homura's mental and emotional state is communicated with symbols and metaphor. The ability to read these symbols and decipher the metaphors can give the viewer a much deeper understanding of what is happening and why. This imagery isn't just a colorful background in front of which the story plays out; it is as much a part of the story as the dialogue, or the action. To dismiss it as window dressing is to miss as much as a third of the message.

DECIPHERING THE RUNES

Just before the epic fight between Homura and Mami, electronic billboards all around the crumbling city advertise Bebe's Sweets. (*Rebellion*, 0:47:31)

ᛉᏇᏐᎡᎩᏐᎩᏞᏚᏗ ᏌᏗᏫ ᎩᏞᎪᏫ:

Of all the hidden messages in *Madoka Magica*, one type stands out, and practically dares the fans to try and understand it. The various symbols which appear so frequently on screen, especially within witch labyrinths are in fact, as they seem, a direct substitution for letters. They can be transliterated to figure out what they say quite easily with the charts presented in this chapter, however, for the first fans to do so, it was quite a challenge.

These symbols, called runes, were originally created by Gekidan Inu Curry (literally Theater Company Dog Curry), who also designed the witches and their labyrinths. In fact, you can probably thank them for most of the visual symbolism which appears in *Rebellion* as well. Rune translations are how we, the fans, came to know the names of all the witches. In every witch scene, the witch's name flashes on screen in runes. Other lines of this runic code

ARCHAIC			
A	ꝺ	P	⚥
B	⊕	Q	☥
C	⨅	R	ɣ
D	ћ	S	⸭
E	☉	T	ʊ
F	ᚠ	U	ℂ
G	◊	V	╲
H	ꞮꞮ	W	Ɜ
I	₰	X	⧞
J	ƅ	Y	ℚ
K	Ӈ	Z	ݐ
L	Ⱡ	Ä	⸚
M	◎	Ö	⸚
N	⁓	Ü	⸚
O	⅋	ß	⸚

also appear, giving us glimpses into the nature of the witch. In *Rebellion*, runes can be seen almost everywhere, especially after Homura begins to suspect that the girls are trapped in a labyrinth. They also make an appearance earlier in the movie during the group transformation scene when the full team fights Hitomi Shizuki's nightmare.

Early attempts to break the code were complicated by inconsistencies, likely intentionally inserted, which made attempts at numerical frequency decoding ineffective. Some of these inconsistencies include unusual spacing, such as adding a space where it doesn't belong or leaving out one where it should have been. Many words are misspelled, and the runes are used to represent three different languages. Japanese, German, and English words appear in runes, further complicating attempts to translate. Finally, there are three distinct fonts for the runes: Modern, Archaic, and Musical.

The archaic font looks more squared off and standardized, like a font you would expect to find in type. The modern font has a more handwritten feel to it, with more rounded edges and gentle curves. The musical font is made up of elements found in musical notes and sheet music, and obviously appears frequently in relation to Sayaka.

The runes were originally translated by western fans. According to trivia posted on IMDB, the fan who originally broke the code was American, but like most IMDB trivia, it does not give any source for the information.[62] Still, during an interview at the US premiere of

---

62. "Puella Magi Madoka Magica trivia," *Internet Movie Data Base*, accessed 29 December 2015, http://www.imdb.com/title/tt1773185/trivia?ref_=tt_trv_trv.

Madoka Magica, producer Atsuhiro Iwakami admitted that the production team was surprised that the runes were cracked by western fans, and stated that even obsessed Japanese fans had not done so.[63] The breakthrough happened when lines of runic script found on screen were compared to quotes from *Faust*. It turned out that the runes were a direct substitution for German letters.[64] These tables are still incomplete, simply because some of the letters were never used on screen so we have no examples. However, if there is another sequel, we may yet see the musical Q or the modern X.

The fact that it was western fans who originally broke the code may explain why English words appear in runes far more often in *Rebellion* than they did in the original series or the recap movies. In fact, in the original series, the runes were used to represent Japanese words or phrases a total of 21 times, German a total of 56 times, and English a total of only 6 times.[65] This comes out to 25.3% Japanese, 67.5% German and 7.2% English. However, in *Rebellion*, we see English appearing in runes 9 times, or 24%, compared to 16 times and 42% for Japanese, and 13 times or 34% for German.

MODERN			
A	𝔇	P	♀
B	●	Q	♉
C	⊞	R	?
D	Π	S	⋮
E	☉	T	☉
F	⊟	U	☾
G	⅃	V	
H	𝔍	W	J
I	♌	X	
J	♭	Y	☊
K	♄	Z	♃
L	♇	Ä	😵
M	☉	Ö	😵
N	☿	Ü	Ĉ
O	♋	ẞ	●

---

63. "Madoka Magica premiere notes," *Puella Magi Wiki*, accessed 19 December 2015, http://wiki.puella-magi.net/Aniplex_USA_Madoka_Premiere.

64. "Deciphering the Runes," *Puella Magi Wiki*, accessed 19 December 2015, http://wiki.puella-magi.net/Deciphering_the_runes.

65. These numbers were determined using the episode by episode transliterations found at www.puella-magi-wiki.net/Deciphering_the_runes. These totals exclude names, such as Charlotte or Homulilly. Only phrases or words which are distinctly Japanese, German or English were counted. There were also a very few instances of musical terms, French and Latin, but these have also been excluded as statistically insignificant.

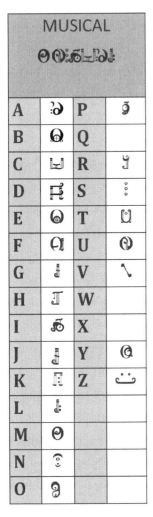

The majority of transliterations are still predominantly Japanese and German, but we see a 33% reduction in German occurrences, and a 17% increase in both Japanese and English.

One could argue that the reason for the shift is that unlike the original series, *Rebellion* is no longer based primarily on *Faust*, but on *The Nutcracker*, most commonly associated with the Russian ballet. However no instances of transliterated Russian appear in *Rebellion*, and the E. T. A. Hoffman version of *The Nutcracker* is still a German novel. Considering that by the time *Rebellion* was animated, the production team knew full well who had cracked the runic code, the addition of so many English phrases could be a tip of the hat to the English speaking fans.

If you are really into crypto linguistics, and want to translate all the runic script found in *Madoka Magica*, please be my guest. Many people find that to be extremely entertaining. However, if you just want to know what it all says, and you don't care to translate it yourself, just visit www.puella-magi-wiki.net/Deciphering_the_runes for an episode by episode translation of practically every instance where a rune appears on screen. This includes the two recap movies, *Rebellion*, and instances where the runes appeared in the various manga. If the transliteration is of a different language, such as German, the wiki page provides the translation in that language as well as in English.

At the end of the *Eternal* movie (1:42:00), after Homura leaps from the building, sprouts angel wings, and fires her bow at the wraiths, the "credits" start to roll, done entirely in runes. In fact the true credits follow the post-credits scene (with Homura in an apparent wasteland). The runic credit scroll is actually messages in transliterated Japanese, with the color of the text indicating which character wrote the message. The majority of these are quotes spoken by the characters during the movie, along with episode titles, which, since all of the episode titles were spoken by a character during that episode, are also quotes. The exception is the text in gray, a single flowing verse which runs the length of the entire scroll. The following page contains the translation of the full scroll. [66]

66. The full translation is found on *Puella Magi Wiki* in the form of an unbroken screen capture with the words translated into English using a font which closely resembles the runes. This image was submitted by user Prima and appears in its entirety on the next page. Accessed 1 Jan 2016, http://wiki.puella-magi.net/File:Runes_Eternal_Story_ED_English.png

There's No Way I'll Ever Regret It

Sayaka trades her soul to heal Kyosuke's hand. (Episode 5, 01:00)

Exploring the Theme of Sacrifice in *Madoka Magica*

Sacrifice is perhaps the central theme of the entire *Madoka Magica* story. To obtain a wish, one must trade their soul. Is the payoff worth the price? Perhaps, but Kyubey's transactions aren't the only form of sacrifice occurring in this story. Each character is an exploration of a different type of sacrifice. Each character gives of themselves in various ways and for various reasons. The notions of selflessness and love are explored, and even the most selfish of characters, Kyoko, started out with a self-sacrificing wish.

Kyoko Sakura

Sacrifice for the Good of the Family

Kyoko's original wish was for people to listen to her father who had started preaching unorthodox sermons and had lost his congregation. Kyoko gave of herself, battling witches every night; risking her own life so that people would come to her father's church and hear his sermons. This is a very straightforward type of sacrifice; the type any of us might make for the ones we love. In fact, most parents make this type of sacrifice; giving of their time to some corporation or government in order to support their families. Here we see it reversed, with the child sacrificing in order to support the parent. It seems like it should work, but it doesn't.

When Kyoko's father finds out that people aren't really interested in his sermons, and that he is not the actual reason for the success he has seen, he becomes angry. There are two reasons for this, and one is because he is a Christian minister. Of what denomination is not clear, but he is definitely Christian. The Bible contains a prohibition against magic, and when he accuses Kyoko of being a witch, this is both ironic in that she is using her powers to fight witches, and accurate in that a magical girl is in fact a nascent witch.

The other reason Kyoko's father rejects her sacrifice is that it is an affront to his ego. He believed that his ideas had stood on their own merits. He thought he had shown his critics that they were wrong, and that he had been right all along. He had found success, and all because of his own efforts and ideas. He was wrong, and he owed everything he had achieved to his daughter, who was using magic to force people to listen and agree with his ideas. He was just as much a failure as he ever was. Compound this failure with the fact that his inability to support his family had even cost his daughter her humanity, and her soul. Kyoko's sacrifice, while well intentioned, only served to highlight her father's incompetence as a priest and as a parent, making him feel even worse than before.

Kyoko's failure was in not understanding her father's needs before she tried to meet them. Had she simply asked her father if he needed help, and what type of help he needed, she may have actually found a wish that would have satisfied the family's needs. This is probably one of the most common failures in any relationship. Too often we assume we know what is best for others, and don't bother to communicate when we should. I am certainly guilty of this. We could all learn something from Kyoko's mistake.

Kyoko's reaction to this is to recoil from sacrifice; rejecting the idea that one can solve other people's problems by giving of yourself. She is of course wrong, but that is the lesson she learns from her mistake. Her focus on self-reliance does have a positive side. It keeps her alive, along with her eating disorder brought about by the lean times when she had no idea where her next meal would come from. Now she can eat as much as she wants, and perhaps that is why her tragedy did not result in her total loss of hope, and her disintegration into a witch. She tries to help Sayaka avoid making the same mistake, but unfortunately for both of them, she is still confused about just what her mistake was.

Sayaka Miki

Sacrifice for Love

Sayaka's sacrifice seems similar to Kyoko's, but it contains a significant difference. She trades her soul, and accepts a future of fighting witches every night in exchange for healing the hand of the boy she loves. The difference here is that Kyosuke is the object of Sayaka's desire. She loves him and wants him to love her back. Where Kyoko would have been happy if her father never found out what she was doing for him, Sayaka's love is different. Her reasons are different. No matter how much she tries to deny it, and no matter how many warnings Mami gives her, she cannot escape the fact that she fully expects to get something for her sacrifice. This is not the familial or storge type of love which Kyoko feels for her father. This is a more personal, individual, desire. This type of romantic love can inspire people to make unbelievable sacrifices, but it is not as selfless because they get something in return. When these feelings are returned, we feel fulfilled, validated, and valued.

One cannot give in this type of relationship without receiving anything in return, or it will eventually empty the vessel which does the giving. This type of relationship needs to be two-way, or one of the partners will eventually have nothing left to give, and those feelings of love and desire can turn to regret and even resentment. We like to pretend that we give to our partner selflessly, but the truth is that it is less of a sacrifice than it seems, because when our partner makes similar sacrifices, the balance is maintained, and neither feels the pain of loss.

Kyosuke's problem, unlike Kyoko's father, is obvious. He cannot play the violin ever again due to an accident which has rendered his hand useless. It's so straightforward. How could Sayaka possibly get this wrong? Like Kyoko, she fails to communicate with the one for whom she intends to sacrifice. This time it is not a misunderstanding of what is needed, and how the other party will react. This time the mistake is in not taking credit for the sacrifice. Sayaka believes that taking credit for healing Kyosuke's hand would be wrong because he will feel indebted to her, and she will never know if he is with her because of love, or guilt. She is right about that part. But in a two-way relationship it is fine to take credit for the things you do to make the other party happy. The problem was that there was no two-way relationship. She had been taking care of him, but he had never made any commitment to her. She should have established the relationship *before* making the sacrifice. That way she would know that he was with her for her, and not because he felt obligated. She could have ruled out that possibility by simply asking him how he felt about her before she gave him the gift. That way his answer would have been honest, and she would not have to worry about whether or not her gift had tainted his response.

We can learn from Sayaka's mistake by understanding that a relationship is all about balance. The two partners in a romantic relationship can be represented by kids on a playground teeter-totter. One can take the majority of the burden, thereby lifting the other up. Over the short term, this can even make the one who carries the burden happy to see their partner happy. It is natural for the burden to shift, and the other partner sinks under the load and thereby raises up the first. If this goes back and forth, neither gets overburdened, and both bring happiness to each other. Sayaka ignored the principle of balance, taking an unimaginable burden for the one she loved. Unfortunately, Kyosuke had not yet sat down on the teeter-totter, and Sayaka simply sank under the weight of the burden she took upon herself, never being lifted up by her partner, who in his defense, never knew he was her partner (although, he probably should have). Sacrifice in a romantic relationship only works when both parties sacrifice. If only one does, the situation will certainly deteriorate.

Mami Tomoe

Service

Or

Sacrifice for Community

When asked about her performance as Mami Tomoe, Carrie Keranen related that she portrayed Mami as, "A helper/mentor/warrior who is deeply lonely. That feeling of wanting to belong somewhere, to someone, the searching for that feeling of 'family' was what I understood and sought to capture."[67]

Mami has no one in her life except for Kyubey. Her parents are dead, and she is partially to blame for that due to her hasty wish. Her apprentice, Kyoko, has left her in order to pursue the dark side of being a magical girl. Mami is desperately lonely. Since she has nobody to sacrifice for, she throws herself into a form of sacrifice for everybody, also known as service. This is the same kind of service which is rendered by the military, police, fire department, or any other first responders who put themselves in harm's way to protect the community. These types of roles are traditionally undervalued and under-paid. This description fits Mami to a T. She didn't even get a wish when she formed her contract. As previously discussed, she could have wished for anything; and surviving her injuries would have been icing on the cake because magical girls cannot die from physical injuries. Mami is a public servant who gets very little in the way of compensation.

She champions justice, fighting to protect the general public; people who will never know who she is or what she has done for them. There is nobody to validate her, to tell her she is doing a good job, to look up to her, or to recognize her sacrifice. At least until Madoka and Sayaka come along. This is why Mami is so happy in the artificial utopia of Homura's witch labyrinth. She is finally the leader of a troop of magical girls; the commander of her unit, no longer alone, and all of her sacrifices are fully recognized and rewarded.

From Mami we can learn that even though service to a cause can be its own reward, we shouldn't throw ourselves entirely into it without getting something in return. Even in service, we should take care of ourselves. We should expect to be rewarded, or at least compensated for our service. If we do not take care of ourselves, we cannot take care of others. Mami serves the community, and she also serves Kyubey. Kyubey is an uncaring and unconcerned user. He takes everything Mami offers, uses her as his champion and recruiter, and gives

67. Carrie Keranen, email interview.

nothing in return. Mami is never paid for her service, not even a wish like the other magical girls received upon making a contract.

Many who enter such services thrive in that culture. They live for recognition in the form of medals, ribbons, praise, and even enhanced position and responsibility. Mami is a classic example of the type of person who fits into a service oriented culture. In *Rebellion* she has achieved exactly this. She is the commander of the squad, setting strategy, giving orders, chastising members for being late, punishing members such as Homura who get out of line, and handing out the rewards, such as cake and tea after a battle if the girls have performed well.

From Mami's example we can see that a balance must be maintained in this form of sacrifice as well. The military is the best example of this type of sacrifice through service. The military culture of "service before self" is demanding, but as with Kyubey, the contract comes with rewards. The military offers benefits in the form of health care, retirement, savings, and education. With any form of service it is important to take advantage of the benefits offered. If not, once that service is concluded, the member may be left with nothing for themselves after years of giving to their community.

Homura Akemi and Madoka Kaname
Self-Sacrifice and Selfish Sacrifice

Homura's form of sacrifice is best viewed when contrasted against Madoka's. They are polar opposites. Homura loves Madoka, and her sacrifice is for Madoka alone. Madoka, on the other hand sacrifices for all. Homura never loses herself, but actually builds herself into a finely tuned weapon in order to get what she wants. Madoka on the other hand is willing to give up everything in exchange for saving others. Homura's strategy is to fight to overpower the system, while Madoka's strategy is to surrender herself to that system. Madoka becomes the system, thereby changing its very nature.

Homura's sacrifice is such that she focuses on saving Madoka to the exclusion of all else. She has no other goals in life. She spends her time gathering weapons, formulating strategies and laying plans. You can hear in her voice that she has had to watch her friends

Homura on the side of a Japanese AH-1 Cobra. Image source: https://wiki.puella-magi.net/File:Nose_art_photo_by_mito.jpg

die so many times that she has become numb inside. The only emotions she expresses are regret over not being able to save Madoka, and occasionally frustration with the other magical girls for not heeding her warnings. She has abandoned the other emotions: empathy, kindness, optimism, etc. She even warns Madoka that these can be fatal flaws for a magical girl. Homura has sacrificed everything in her life except those things which enable her to attain her goal. She has spent approximately a decade of her life working to save Madoka.

There's a reason why many anime fans in the military find Homura to be a kind of inspiration. She is an expert with every type of weapon, and will do whatever it takes to complete her mission. She is unstoppable and has a will of iron. Her duty to Madoka comes first, everything else is secondary. With her single minded dedication to a cause, dazzling competency and overwhelming firepower, it's no wonder the Fourth Anti-Tank Helicopter Squadron of the Japanese Ground Self Defense Force put her image on the side of a Cobra attack helicopter.[68]

Homura started as weak, unskilled, and unsure of herself. By the end she had transformed herself into the strongest, most powerful, most skilled and confident magical girl. Self-improvement, loyalty, strength, confidence, competence, and endurance are all elements which appeal to the military culture.

The core of Homura's sacrifice is related to her nature as a magical girl. She is the

---

68. The 4th Anti-tank Helicopter Squadron may call her Aoi-chan, and claim that she is an original character drawn by members of the squadron, but considering her similarities to Homura, including eye color, hair style and headband, and the fact that *Madoka Magica* aired ten months before Aoi joined the squadron, there is more than enough reason to speculate that Aoi was inspired by Homura. "The Four Sisters of the Fourth Anti-Tank Helicopter Squad are Celebrated One Last Time!" *Tokyo Otaku Mode*, accessed 21 December 2015, http://otakumode.com/news/51a149bf8ccdf39e1300d1e4/The-Four-Sisters-of-the-Fourth-Anti-Tank-Helicopter-Squad-are-Celebrated-One-Last-Time!.

magical girl of time, and time is what she gives. If we only consider the on-screen events, then she has given perhaps half a year in the effort to save Madoka. If we consider Gen Urobuchi's comments, then she has given perhaps as much as a decade. From Homura, we can take inspiration. She may be a fictional character, but her dedication to Madoka is nonetheless moving. Wouldn't we all want a friend like her? Could any of us ever be such a friend, or lover?

Madoka takes the whole series to make her decision. She listens to Homura's warnings, Mami's encouragement, and she learns from Sayaka's mistake. Madoka, unlike Mami, takes the time to think things through and doesn't just wish to get herself, or Homura out of a bad situation. She gets all of the magical girls out of that situation. Unlike Mami, Madoka does not thrive on praise or recognition. Unlike Sayaka, she is not fixated on a single individual. Unlike Kyoko, she listens to the needs of her intended recipients. Unlike Homura, she is willing to let go of everything in order to achieve the perfect solution. In exchange, nothing of herself remains; not even the memory of her existence. Madoka's sacrifice is total. She gives everything of herself to get that one thing that she wants more than anything else. She sacrifices herself to save the ones she cares about. But don't worry, in the end, Homura will even protect Madoka from herself. After all, Homura's wish wasn't really about sacrifice, it was about power.[69]

However, as Christina Vee points out, Homura's wish for power may have been an attempt to exploit a loophole in the rules of Magica style karma. As we know, a wish for someone else invariably ends in disaster, and Homura may have picked up on this by watching what happened to Sayaka and Kyoko. Cristina Vee says Homura didn't simply wish Madoka back to life because she didn't want her wish to end up like Sayaka's wish for Kyosuke. Instead of making a wish for someone else, she made a wish that granted her incredible power, and then used that power to help Madoka.[70]

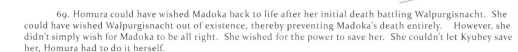

69. Homura could have wished Madoka back to life after her initial death battling Walpurgisnacht. She could have wished Walpurgisnacht out of existence, thereby preventing Madoka's death entirely. However, she didn't simply wish for Madoka to be all right. She wished for the power to save her. She couldn't let Kyubey save her, Homura had to do it herself.

70. Cristina Vee, email correspondence with the author, 29 June 2016.

Color Coded for Your Convenience[71]

The team assembles to battle Hitomi's nightmare. (*Rebellion*, 0:21:00)

It sure is easy to keep all the characters in *Madoka Magica* straight. Their hair color matches their eye color, which matches their costume color. Even before you know their names, you know the pink girl is friends with the blue girl, and the purple girl is very mysterious. Still, the costumes and the colors serve a greater purpose than just helping the viewer keep track of who's who.

Actually, it's standard procedure in mahou shoujo anime to color code the team members. There are actually three reasons for this: Tradition, Marketing, and Symbolism. Let's start out by looking at the evolution of the genre.

---

71. Sonnenberg's sarcastic yet glowing review of the original series includes the line, "The girls are all color coded for your convenience." *SF Debris* review, Madoka Magica Episode 1.

The tradition of color coding magical girls began with *Sailor Moon*. Actually, *Sailor Moon* was the first mahou shoujo anime to become internationally popular, but it was also the first to put together all the tropes which we associate with magical girls in the genre as we know it today. But *Sailor Moon* was certainly not the first magical girl anime.

Let's follow *Madoka Magica*'s family tree back to its roots. If we go all the way back, we will find that the true root of all magical girls was actually Samantha Stevens. That's right, from the American T.V. series *Bewitched*. Two different anime/manga series were either inspired, or directly adapted from Bewitched: *Mahoutsukai Sally* (*Sally the Witch*) and *Himitsu no Akko-chan* (*Secrets of Akko-chan*).[72][73] Not only are these the first to appear, but they also represent the first branch of the tree. With these two anime, we see a split in the types of magical girls. Type one, the Sally type, are naturally magical, and are likely to be a princess from a magical world who is just visiting our normal world. Type two, the Akko type, receive their powers from a magical item or creature.[74]

The anime *Cutie Honey* represents yet another branch on the way to *Madoka Magica*. *Cutie Honey* introduced the idea of the magical girl warrior, where the girl transforms in order to do battle with the forces of evil.[75] Magical girls not of this branch transformed into older versions of themselves, or other people such as pop idols. *Sailor Moon* certainly falls into the warrior branch. Not only that, *Sailor Moon* made use of the magical girl team, a feature which it did not invent, but that it arguably perfected. And of course, since you have several similarly dressed heroines, you need a way to tell them apart, especially on the toy store shelf.

72. Sugawa Akiko, "Children of Sailor Moon: The Evolution of Magical Girls in Japanese Anime," *Nippon.com, Your Doorway to Japan*, accessed 23 December 2015, www.nippon.com/en/a03904/.

73. "Magical Girl," *TV Tropes*, accessed 23 December 2015, http://tvtropes.org/pmwiki/pmwiki.php/Main/MagicalGirl.

74. Sugawa.

75. "The Origin and Evolution of Magical Girls," *Anime Amino*, accessed 23 December 2015, http://aminoapps.com/page/anime/1118114/origin-and-evolution-of-magical-girls.

The bonds between the animation and toy industries are strong, and not just here in the U.S. where animated T.V. shows are often nothing more than 30 minute long toy commercials. Even when an anime is not aimed at the young, traditionally toy-buying demographic, the market for models, figures, plushies, etc. is significant. Practically all anime, including those for older or mature audiences are well represented in collectible merchandise. If you need any proof of this, just visit the dealer's room of any con.

The studios color code the animated characters for marketing purposes. How do you sell three times as many robot lions, transforming airplanes, dolls, action figures, etc.? Easy, make a blue version, a green version, and of course a pink one for the girls. In many cases you don't even have to change the design of the toy, just make it a different color. That may have been the original reason for color coding magical girls, but these days with the extreme quality of figures sold you would be able to tell them apart even without the color coding. But we also can't discount the influence of the super sentai shows popular around the same time as *Sailor Moon*, from whom the idea was likely borrowed. Still, I would imagine that in the dark it is difficult to tell the red power ranger action figure from the black one.

So there you have it, the evolutionary tree which led to *Madoka Magica*. What we have is a magical girl anime in the Akko tradition with the girls having no innate magical powers and having to obtain their powers from a magical creature. They transform into magical warriors to fight "evil," in the *Cutie Honey* tradition. They fight (sometimes) as a color coded team in the *Sailor Moon* tradition. But there is still more to it than that.

Madoka Magica goes a little farther than just giving each girl a different color. All the girls in *Sailor Moon* wore pretty much identical outfits in different colors. The magical girls in *Madoka Magica* however, have dramatically different costumes in their magical girl forms. This allows for the designer to add another layer to the code. Now it is possible to make each costume resemble something the audience is familiar with, adding a subliminal effect which cues us in to the nature of the character.

Of course Mars is the red planet, so Sailor Mars had to wear a red costume. Pretty simple, right? Not so fast. Rei Hino, was a Shinto shrine maiden in her mundane life, I mean, when she wasn't wearing a sailor suit. And shrine maidens wear a white kimono top with a red hakama. The hakama is an extremely wide pair of pleated pants, which pretty much looks exactly like a skirt. So, Sailor Mars' white topped, red skirted sailor guardian uniform reflects her role in real life just as much as it does the planet for which she is named.

We can see this same type of pattern in *Madoka Magica*. Kyoko is the red magical girl, but she isn't a shrine maiden. Still, this is a very strong subliminal message to send to, in particular, a Japanese audience. Sure, Kyoko's father was apparently a Christian minister of some type, but the basics are the same. The red magical girl is still assisting a priest in a religious institution. Not only that, but it is common in Japanese fiction for shrine maidens to have magical powers. If you thought "shrine maiden" when you first saw Kyoko in her magical girl costume, you were pretty close to the truth. Just change shrine to church and Shinto to Christianity and you've hit the nail right on the head. If you must use a strictly Christian element for the reference, then go with a cardinal, either way, the color fits.

Sayaka's blue costume has several messages. Obviously, blue brings up thoughts of water, and she is closely tied to the *Little Sea-Maid*, so it works on that level. Cool blue water to match Kyoko's fiery red. Also, she wears a cape, the signature accoutrement of a hero, which is how she sees herself, at least at first. Finally, her weapon is the sword, which conjures an image of a knight or crusader, again aptly describing her character.

Madoka is the girliest and cutest of the characters. In fact, Umi Aoki, the character designer for the show said, "Madoka was drawn to be the very image of a magical girl. I added almost fairy tale-ish hints, so hopefully female viewers will be charmed by her as well...Full of tiny frills, with ribbons arranged at the neck, waist, and on the shoes. It's perfectly 'cute,' and seemingly unsuited for combat, but..."[76] There may be more to it.

[76]. Ume Aoki, "Design Notes," *Megami*, January 2011. Translation at: *Puella Magi Wiki*, accessed 23 December 2015, https://wiki.puella-magi.net/Megami_Magazine_2011-01.

Madoka is a young angel of mercy, volunteering to take away the suffering of others. There is a traditionally pink angel of mercy in real life, with attributes of youth usually ascribed to the role. The hospital volunteer. This author could not help but think of a candy striper when confronted by the pink and white of Madoka's costume. Was the resemblance intentional? Who can say? But the subliminal message was received loud and clear, and quite accurate too considering the nature of her character.

Mami wears a yellow, quite obviously German inspired costume, and uses rifled muskets as her weapon. In Ume Aoke's own words, "Mami's design was definitely centered around her image as a gunner. The second thing that stands out are her breasts. Her bustier and boots give her a Western flavor which her cap accentuates."[77] German rifle troops during the 1700s were called Jägers. The term Jäger, meaning hunter, was probably a reference to their weapon since at that time the rifle was primarily seen as a hunting weapon. The British were still exclusively using smooth bore muskets at the time. But Mami is a hunter of sorts too. She scouts out and recruits new magical girls. Kyubey identifies the girls with potential, and Mami moves in to sell the magical girl deal. So Mami as a hunter is an apt metaphor.

But what about Homura's costume? It looks even more like a school uniform than her school uniform. What could it possibly represent? The answer lies in the Japanese name for that particular style of school uniform, "sera fuku." Sera fuku is a phrase adapted from English, even if it is hard to recognize. It was originally "sailor suit," referring to a naval uniform. So, it is certainly appropriate that the magical girl who uses military weaponry as her primary offensive skill wears a costume inspired by a military uniform.

A red costume for the religious girl, a caped sword-weilding blue knight, a young angel of mercy decked in pink and white, a rifle toting hunter, and a military specialist complete with uniform. You can learn a lot about these characters just by looking at their clothes.

77. Ibid.

Deconstructing the Magical Girl

Girl, Soul Jem, Sugar, Pepper Sauce, Dream, Hope, Innocence (a small quantity). Please be careful about the handling of the magic.[78]

If you knew nothing whatsoever about *Madoka Magica* before watching it, then I applaud you. You got the best possible viewing experience, with no spoilers to ruin the surprises which are the best part of the show. But just about everyone has heard that this series is a deconstruction of the magical girl genre. That alone isn't too much of a spoiler, but if you know what a deconstruction is, it will trigger certain expectations.

What is a deconstruction? A deconstruction is when a story takes the unnatural, yet for some reason unquestioned and fully accepted elements of a genre, and plays them out as if they happened in the real world. The point is to show that despite what you see in the average *Superman* movie, absolute power does corrupt absolutely. It attempts to show how a normal person would react to having unusual abilities, responsibilities, etc., thrust upon them. Great examples include *Hancock* in the live action superhero genre, and *Neon Genesis Evangelion* in

78. Apparent recipe for a "Mahou Syoujo," from transliterated runes found in *Rebellion* during Nagisa Momoe's transformation scene. Off to the side, an image of Charlotte/Bebe says, "Sweet." (1:25:37).

shonen mecha anime. These shows ask the questions of the genre which are inconvenient to ask in a normal series of that type, and it pulls at the strings which normally get overlooked. Of course, pulling at those strings causes the situation to unravel, and that is what we get in a deconstruction.

Madoka Magica asks the questions which other mahou shoujo anime normally skip over, such as: Where did that furry animal handing out superpowers come from? Why is he handing these powers out? What does he get from the deal? Nothing is free, so what is the cost of gaining these powers? How would a teenage girl respond to the pressure of life-or-death combat? How would she be able to bear the pressure of being responsible for literally saving the world? How would others react to finding out what she is? How would it affect her social life? What is she fighting for, and if it is valuable, would the others try to take it from her?

Madoka Magica contains all the trappings of the genre, but it is deliberately disrespectful to them. It turns the normally helpful and hopeful nature of the magical girl troupe on its head, as well as the relationship with the furry little animal who is usually the helper. Additionally, magical girls are supposed to be incorruptible heroines, not morally reprehensible, as Kyoko Sakura surely is. Magical girls are supposed to be strong, but many of *Madoka Magica*'s characters are weak, fragile, flawed, realistic human characters. Let's take a look at the various aspects of mahou shoujo anime which *Madoka Magica* deconstructs.

The Helpful Animal Familiar

Kyubey is to *Madoka Magica* what Luna is to *Sailor Moon*, or Yuno is to *Lyrical Nanoha*, etc. It is a standard feature of magical girl anime in the Akko tradition that some cute, small, animal befriends the girl and grants her magical powers. Kyubey does this, but what all of these other shows fail to address is why the little critters seem to always choose middle school girls. Heck, Nanoha is only nine! Actually, it seems a fairly altruistic and very trusting thing to do, giving incredible powers to these very young girls.

Madoka Magica asks the question, and gives a very good answer. The heroic and friendly familiar has been made into the ultimate villain, even a predator. He preys on the girls because of their naiveté, harnessing their emotional energy and eventually consuming their very souls.

They are easy targets, all too willing to trust a cute, furry, innocent looking little creature handing out super powers and cute costumes. Cassandra Lee Morris plays Kyubey. She says, "Kyubey is a very one-dimensional character. I modeled him after a slimy used-car salesman who knows he's cute."[79]

Kyubey is a monster, but somehow he seems more realistic than the other magical girl familiars because Kyubey is behaving out of self-interest. This makes sense because it is consistent with what we would expect from an alien creature who stalks the young and the innocent. He is definitely getting something out of the deal. He's basically doing the same thing as Luna, using the girls to save something of value. In Luna's case it was to fight evil and defeat the Dark Kingdom. In comparison, Kyubey's goal seems even nobler than Luna's. After all, Kyubey is trying to save the entire universe. In his judgment, the end justifies the means. The needs of the many outweigh the needs of the few. So what if he has to kill off the human race,[80] as long as the rest of the universe can be saved.

The Incorruptible Hero

The incorruptible heroine is the staple of the magical girl genre. Sure, Usagi is likely to chicken out of facing off with a particularly scary threat, but that's not the same as having a real character flaw like Kyoko. Kyoko actually allows innocent people to die in order to get the grief seeds she needs to sustain herself. She has been through a traumatic past, and has suppressed the memories of those events even to the point of losing one of her magical powers, the power of illusion.[81] She makes up for the lack of magical ability by ratcheting up the violence of her physical attacks.

While we are on the topic of violence, here we find another major difference. The typical magical girl uses a wand. After all, she is fighting a magical battle. However, in *Madoka*

---

79. Cassandra Lee Morris, email interview conducted by the author, 6 May 2016.

80. Kyubey knows full well that if Madoka makes a contract she will become the most powerful magical girl ever, and eventually the most wicked of witches. When this comes to pass, he proclaims that she will destroy the entire world in less than a week, but blows it off as "humanity's problem." He has gathered all the energy he needs, and no longer cares what happens to the humans. (Episode 10, 21:56)

81. It is revealed in the *Different Story* manga that Kyoko used to have the power to make her adversary see whatever she wanted, no doubt this is because her original wish was to deceive people.

Magica, where the threat posed to the girls by the witches is very physical, so are their weapons. The wand has been exchanged for more tangible, or believable weapons. The gun, sword, spear, and bow are the constant companions of these magical warriors.

Homura, like Kyoko, is emotionally scarred. She has watched Madoka die so many times she doesn't feel anything anymore, even going so far as to kill, or at least attempt to kill other magical girls if they get in the way. If Kyoko had not intervened, she surely would have killed Sayaka. There is no doubt that if saving Madoka meant all the other girls had to die, she would be fine with that. When Madoka asks her to use her power to save the others, Homura becomes angry with Madoka, telling her that she doesn't have enough power to save everyone, she can only save Madoka. She scolds Madoka, telling her, "Don't ever tell me not to save you."[82] For Homura, the entire world can burn, so long as Madoka is saved.

Mami is presenting the world the way we expect it to be. She is flashy, heroic, team oriented and righteous. She almost certainly believes the lie she is selling. She is both tricking the audience as much as the prospective magical girls, because the author is using her to play into our, the viewer's, expectations. This is so the story can pull the rug out from under us once we have been lulled into a false sense of security born of familiarity. This is the setup for the sucker punch.

Mami is clearly operating at the very extent of her emotional limits. She was probably aware that something wasn't quite right, but has been telling herself that Kyubey is family, or at least the closest thing she has to family. She has been totally loyal to him, even recruiting new magical girls for him. When confronted with the truth of Kyubey's deception, her fragile world falls apart and she is confronted by the reality that she is the personal assistant of a monster. She has become part of a system for turning girls into witches so Kyubey can consume their souls. Her response is to kill the other girls to prevent them from turning into witches. She would have succeeded, had she not underestimated Madoka, who shot and killed

82. Mura Kuroe, *Puella Magi Oriko Magica*, Vol 2, Magica Quartet, (New York: Yen Press, 2013) 79-80.

her first.

These are not the super heroes of the typical magical girl anime, they are characters who respond to the situation in a way which is believable based on their limited life experience. How else is a middle school girl supposed to deal with the fact that she is responsible for saving the world, and will certainly die in the performance of that duty. They do it by finding something to hold onto. They need something to focus on to give them the strength to go out and stare death in the face night after night. For Sayaka it is Kyosuke and her heroic persona and sense of justice. For Mami it is companionship. For Kyoko it is food. For Homura it is Madoka. Threaten those things, and the girl is likely to respond as if her very life is threatened, and in a very real sense it is.

The Team

Anime such as *Sailor Moon* emphasize the importance of contributing to the team. Any one of the girls is rarely able to handle the episode's challenge, but when all of them face it together, it is overcome. *Madoka Magica* incorporates an element which defeats teamwork. Each witch only drops one grief seed. Only one reward, no matter how many girls risk their lives to get it. The more girls on the team, the more you have to ration the rewards, making it unprofitable to team up, to the point where magical girls will fight each other over territory. Kyoko tries to incapacitate Sayaka in order to take control of Mitakihara City, apparently a prime hunting ground. When it becomes obvious that Sayaka can withstand physical injury, Kyoko decides to kill her instead. The idea of teamwork has turned into bitter competition. This is part of what Madoka sees as being wrong with the world. She often remarks that this isn't how it's supposed to be, and that is why the wraiths drop multi-part grief seeds after she makes her wish and becomes the Law of Cycles.

Madoka Magica takes those elements which we take for granted in the genre and shines a light of reality on them. Nobody is going to risk their life unless there is something in it worth the risk, and if it's worth that much, it is probably something worth fighting to protect. This drives the heroes, who are actually providing a valuable service to society, and are therefore worthy of the name, to become less than perfect. These imperfections, such as fighting amongst each other, contribute to their already significant emotional problems stemming from their often tragic circumstances which led them to become magical girls in the first place. All in all, it is very logical, believable, and realistic. But inserting that realism into the normally overlooked holes in the magical girl formula causes it to fall apart, replacing hope with despair and heroics with necessity.

Moments
The Theme of Balance in *Madoka Magica*

Sayaka shows Kyoko her darkened soul gem, admitting she finally understands the concept of balance, but it's too late. (Episode 8, 21:30)

> Balance means good and bad have to zero themselves out, right? That's what you said. Or something like it. I think I understand what you mean now. The good thing is I did save a few people. But the bad thing is, I got angry and my heart filled up with envy and hate. It got so bad, I even hurt my best friend. For all the happiness you wish for someone, someone else gets cursed with equal misery. That's how it works for magical girls, and that's how it is for me. I was stupid, so stupid!
> -Sayaka Miki

Madoka Magica balances everything out to give us an outstandingly well structured story. Good is balanced against evil, cuteness is balanced against darkness, realism is balanced against fantasy, and hope is balanced against despair. The idea of balance is of course central to the idea of wishes, and explains why they ultimately end in disaster. The story is also balanced in its narrative design, with episodes mirroring each other so that we don't get all the good stuff at one end, or have characters that get more attention than others.

Balance in Narrative Structure

The series was very carefully designed to ensure that each character got a balanced treatment. A few episodes were devoted to each. Sayaka and Madoka, although present from the first episode, are given their own arcs, with Sayaka's starting in episode four, when she becomes a magical girl, and ending in episode eight, when she becomes a witch. Her story focuses on her relationship with Kyosuke, who was hardly even mentioned before episode three. Madoka acts primarily as an observer through which we witness the events of the series, although she does get some development throughout. She doesn't really become the central character until the final two episodes when she finally takes on the role of savior. Kyoko first appears in episode four, but her story really starts in five when she attempts to take over Mami's former territory from Sayaka, and of course her story is focused on her relationship with Sayaka, rocky as it is. Kyoko's arc ends at episode nine, when she sacrifices herself to end Sayaka's suffering. Mami is given the first three episodes, and Homura is given the last three, but wow did they shine in the episodes they were given, being practically the sole focus of those episodes. Three episodes for Mami and Homura, and five each for Kyoko and Sayaka, two for Madoka. For a twelve episode series, it is remarkable that it was designed in a way that we get full development from all five main characters. Few series, even those twice as long, ever achieve this. But there's more to the balance of this story than its treatment of the characters.

  The show is balanced in its overall structure. The first two episodes of the original series are basically a two part episode running together quite naturally, and both serving to present the false pretense that this is a cookie cutter, happy-go-lucky, typical magical girl show. Nothing particularly heavy or shocking happens in these two episodes, although there is plenty of foreshadowing if the viewer is paying attention. The last two episodes, in which Homura faces off against Walpurgisnacht, are also a two-parter. The last two episodes are honest, and present the world of *Madoka Magica* as it really is, all plot twists fully revealed. These two part episodes serve as book ends and bracket the rest of the story. As we move in from the ends, we get to another symmetrical pattern.

  Both the third episode and the third from last episode contain momentous revelations. In episode three we are jolted from the false pretenses of the lighthearted setup by the death of Mami Tomoe. Through Mami's death we learn just how dangerous this magical girl business really is. Likewise, episode ten is where we learn the truth about Homura, and how she has been turning back time again and again to try to save Madoka. This revelation is transformational as well, finally confirming Homura as the hero, where she had originally been presented as the villain.

The next point of symmetry comes in episodes six and seven, which straddle the half way point of the story. Episode six starts off with a bit of exposition by Kyubey as he explains how grief seeds are used to cleanse soul gems, and we also learn that Kyubey consumes the grief seeds once they are used up, establishing his role as a predator. Sayaka is filled with pride about being a magical girl. Her only regret is that she didn't become one sooner. She is visited by Kyoko, who takes her somewhere private so they can fight to the death, but it is broken up by Madoka throwing Sayaka's gem off the bridge. The girls learn the truth about their soul gems. At least, they learn that their souls have been removed from their body and placed in the gem. They are basically immortal so long as they maintain the gem, and they will collapse and die without it. You could say, this is the central issue of the entire story.

Episode seven also starts off with more exposition on the part of Kyubey, but this time it is much darker, as he tortures Sayaka to teach her how her soul gem protects her from physical injury. Again, Kyoko pays Sayaka a visit, but this time it is not to fight. This time, Kyoko reaches out and tries to befriend Sayaka. It is apparent from the way Sayaka hesitates that no matter what she says, she does actually have regrets about her decision. She even confesses to Madoka that she considered how things would be if she hadn't saved Hitomi. This is not the same Sayaka from the previous episode; proud, and sure of herself and her ideals. This is a conflicted Sayaka, doubting herself and her choices. Now, she is ashamed of herself. These episodes are mirror images of each other. And like a reflection, they are opposites.

Miracles Aren't Free

> Miracles aren't free you know. If you wish for something good to happen a whole lot of bad stuff's gonna happen too. I guess that's how the world stays in balance. Good, bad, everything zeros out.
> Kyoko Sakura, (Episode seven, 12:09)

The concept of wishes is also based on balance, or perhaps even on karma. For every bit of joy which the wish brings, it will also produce the same amount of sorrow. As Kyubey points out, wishes disrupt the natural order of things, and the universe reacts to restore that balance.

That is why Madoka had to disappear, forgotten by even her family. The universe couldn't just give her what she asked for, it had to take something in return. This also explains why Mami was able to survive so long. She never got a wish, because wishing to live is pointless when the very act of making a contract restores your body to perfect health. Mami's only despair came from forgetting to include her parents in her salvation.

In the final analysis, it is even fitting that the girl who is granted a wish will ultimately die for it. Homura points this out clearly; a wish is worth a life.

> Madoka: Why would Kyubey do something so cruel to us?
> Homura: But it doesn't think of it as cruel. It is a form of life that cannot comprehend human values. It would probably insist that it is simply fair payment for the miracles it grants.
> Madoka: But it isn't a fair exchange at all! To have that done to her body when all she wanted was to heal the wounds of the boy she loved!
> Homura: That doesn't change the fact that it was a miracle. Because it made something impossible possible. Even if Sayaka had spent her entire life caring for him, that boy never would have regained the ability to perform.
> In truth, the value of a miracle is far greater than an entire human life.
> And it is that which that creature sells.
> *(Beginnings Story, 1:33:13)*

This theme of balancing good and evil can likely be traced back to the idea of karma, referenced by Kyubey on many occasions; karmic destiny, karmic potential, etc. The concept of karma is found in nearly all of the world's religions. It is basically the idea that your actions have consequences, and that if you do good or evil, they will eventually come back to affect you. This is seen in the Christian tradition by the phrase, "As you sow, so shall you reap," from Galatians IV. The Buddhist tradition takes it even farther. Not only do your current actions affect you, but your circumstances in this life may be determined by your actions in a previous life. When Mami says, "The motive behind a wish is what matters most,"(episode 3, 05:30) this is the quintessential Buddhist view of karma. But that's not how magica karma works. With magica karma, the more good you do, the more bad has to happen to balance it out. In *Madoka Magica*, the universe is running a zero sum game. If you put a certain amount of good on one side of the equation, the universe has to add the same amount of bad on the other side to balance it out. It is actually a corruption of the idea of karma that turns it on its head. However, it does explain why bad things happen to good people. It's just the universe maintaining its balance.

Opposites

The theme of balance also includes the sub-category of opposites. Opposites balance out afterall, and *Madoka Magica* is full of opposites. In fact, most elements of the story start as one thing, and end up as the opposite.

The most obvious example of this idea is the way the series was presented by SHAFT. Prior to its airing, and indeed all the way up until the infamous third episode, the series creators continued to present the false impression that *Madoka Magica* was a typical, light and happy slice of life anime with a magical girl theme. Once the third episode was out there, and the story started to turn darker and more serious, they dropped the happy kid's show pretense, as it had become apparent that this was anything but.

By the title of the show, one would expect Madoka to be the hero, or at least the main character. For the first couple of episodes, it seems to be headed in that direction. Admittedly, the audience experiences the story from her perspective, but she is mostly relegated to the role of an observer who only steps in to save the day at the very last minute. That is not to diminish her as a character. She has genuinely heroic moments, like when she throws the bucket of chemicals out the window to prevent the mass suicide in episode four. She is also very thoughtful, gathering all the facts before making her decision. She is an intelligent, patient, genuinely good character, but she is still mostly an observer to the majority of the action.

Sayaka initially comes off as very strong, and sure of herself. She is the most eager to make a contract, even bringing a baseball bat on their first witch hunt. But only days later she has completely given in to despair, lost all faith in humanity, and given up on her vision of following in Mami's footsteps as a champion of justice. The girl who seems to be the strongest and bravest is the one who gives up the easiest; the one who cannot bear the emotional burden of being a magical girl. She also gives us an opportunity to examine just how closely the two opposites of selflessness and selfishness are truly related. Her wish, on the surface, looked like the ultimate act of self sacrifice, but even when we give freely, we can have a hard time letting go of the expectation that it will be reciprocated. She shows us that there is such a hing as selfish giving.

Kyoko is the exact opposite of Sayaka. She is truly resilient. Sh[e ...] worse than Sayaka, and she keeps on going. But while she seems stro[ng ...] has been wounded the deepest. So much so that she repressed the tragic events of her past to the point of completely forgetting her magical power, the power of illusion. According to the *Different Story* manga, Kyoko initially had the power to make her opponents see whatever she wanted. This is surely related to her wish, in which people were made to believe her father's sermons. However, after the death of her family, she completely forgets, or at least never again uses this power. Unlike Sayaka, who surrenders to the tragedies and despair brought on by her contract, Kyoko puts the past behind her, copes with it in her own way, and presses on with conviction. She is powerful, even without her illusions, and driven. She won't let anything get in her way. And although she is initially presented as the most selfish, she ends up dying for someone else.

One of the more enjoyable juxtapositions was the contrast of hero vs. villain. Homura was initially presented as the mysterious, even dangerous potential villain. She opposed the obviously heroic and seemingly innocent Kyubey and Mami. She seemed to be dedicated to stopping Madoka from taking her expected place as the hero of the story. By the end, however, the tables had completely turned, and we see that Homura's opposition to Kyubey was fully justified, even heroic, and she was only protecting Madoka all along.

Kyubey on the other hand, is initially presented as harmless, even altruistic, but turns out to be the most dangerous and self-centered character in the whole story. He is deceptive. While he avoids outright lying to the girls, he definitely bends the truth nearly to the breaking point, and withholds vital information which he knows would be important to the girls. He never tells them what the contract entails; that it will lead to certain death, whether by witches, or by other magical girls. He manipulates the girls into fighting each other in order to tempt Madoka into making a contract. He engineers a situation where all the other girls are dead, save Homura, and Madoka must make a contract or watch her friend die fighting a hopeless battle. In episode ten, he even directly causes the destruction of the entire planet, n only say, "Its humanity's problem now." He has a quota to fill, and misery is the fastest way to fill it. However, not everyone sees Kyubey as completely evil.

Cassandra Lee Morris has an interesting take on Kyubey as a character, and as a villain. "Kyubey plays the villain of *Madoka Magica*, but he's not a villain at his core. He's an incubator," says Morris. "Kyubey doesn't experience human emotions the way that humans do. I believe that you can't fully understand something unless you can fully experience it yourself. Therefore, I don't think Kyubey understands the girls' distress or why they are upset."

"Kyubey may observe the girls being upset, but since he has never experienced it and can't relate to it, he doesn't understand what they are going through. A tear, an agonized scream or a face twisted with grief and despair all mean nothing to him. Kyubey isn't capable of laughing or crying, his face doesn't emote (heck, his mouth doesn't even move) and his tone remains even in every interaction with another being. He has no emotions therefore he can't understand emotions. He truly has a one-track mind, and is solely focused on his mission of keeping the universe running."

"He knows he is ending the girls' existences as a human being, but his contracts are perfectly justifiable to him: he's granting them a wish and turning them into a powerful magical girl. Plus, is it his fault the girls made a contract without reading the fine print? Nope."[83]

Mami Tomoe, like all the rest of the characters initially appears to be one thing, but by the end she is revealed to be the opposite. Mami first appears when she comes to the rescue of Madoka and Sayaka as they run from Homura and end up in a witch labyrinth. This valiant entrance sets Mami up as the hero of the story. As the story progresses, she is presented as a champion of justice. However on a second viewing we see her in a completely different light. She is Kyubey's most loyal companion; his recruiter and cheerleader. She seeks out new girls and brings them into Kyubey's influence. She encourages new girls to become magical girls and make contracts. None of this causes the slightest bit of suspicion on the first viewing,

---

83. Cassandra Morris, email interview.

but a couple of episodes after her death, Kyubey's true nature is revealed. He is literally praying on the girls Mami recruits; causing their suffering and eventually devouring their souls, supposedly as part of his plan to save the universe. Mami is the right hand of the story's villain. Arguably, that makes her, the character initially presented as the hero, to be a villian as well. At the very least, she aids the villain. But lets not forget that she is ignorant of Kyubey's true nature. Carrie Keranen reminds us that:

"I don't know that Mami knows of Kyubey what we learn. For Mami, Kyubey has been like a parent and with that comes good and bad stuff but the belief that the intention is always for the best. She was deeply lonely and he was her only friend. So, I am not sure I would consider her a hero or villain based on her relationship with Kyubey specifically. I think...as a mentor and a person who has been knocked around in the world and has lost the ability to stand inside a black and white existence, the world is shades of grey and only children (Madoka and Sayaka at the beginning) have the luxury of believing in right and wrong. As they go along, they discover the complexities of the adult world full of grey."[84]

One more example of things appearing as their own opposite can be found in the dialogue. Several times in *Madoka Magica* the lightest of lines carry the heaviest weight. For example, in episode one when Madoka, Sayaka and Hitomi are eating together after school and Madoka tells how she first saw Homura during a dream, the other two girls laugh at her and throw out seemingly ridiculous suggestions about how they must have met in a different lifetime, or that Madoka actually did meet Homura before, and retains some subconscious memory of her. Both suggestions seem to be throwaway lines, poking fun at stereotypical anime plot lines, yet both turn out to be literally true. Instead of simple small talk, they are actually meaningful foreshadowing.

Another example can be found in episode four, when Madoka and Homura walk together after leaving the late Mami's apartment. Madoka can see that Homura is envious when

---

84. Carrie Keranen, email interview.

Madoka emphatically declares that she will never forget Mami or her sacrifice. She adds, as an afterthought, that she will never forget Homura either. It's the kind of thing any of us would have added, and it certainly doesn't seem terribly deep or thought provoking. However, Homura's reaction to the line tells us that there is more to it. She becomes visibly distressed, and leaves. Like the previous example, this too becomes clear on the second viewing. The truth is that Madoka has already forgotten Homura, her very best friend. As far as Madoka knows, they only met a few days ago. From Homura's perspective, they have known each other for years.

Of course, the symmetry found in the endings of the original story and *Rebellion* makes an outstanding set of bookends. The original series ended with the fully selfless wish on the part of Madoka, which unintentionally had the consequence of robbing Homura of her wish. Madoka gave up everything to save the magical girls as a whole from the fate of turning into witches. It was a strong ending which wrapped up the story nicely, with one exception; Homura still had not been paid for her contract. She had not yet been able to protect Madoka. Madoka saved herself. This ending contrasts nicely with the ending of *Rebellion* in which Homura demands payment for her selfish, but justified wish, and intentionally overrides Madoka's. She wished to re-do her meeting with Madoka, but to have the power to protect her. That is exactly how *Rebellion* ends. An equally strong ending, but one that demands payment, rather than giving up everything. Both, however, eloquently bring closure to the story, even though there was plenty of hinting that there will probably be more to come.

Epilogue

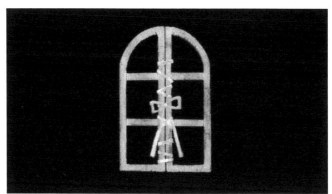

Final image from the end of *Rebellion*. The ribbon ties the window shut. There is no escape from this dream. (1:56:03)

Much of what I have offered here is my own personal interpretation of the world of *Madoka Magica*. As Jed Blue astutely points out, we cannot know for sure what is in the heart of the writer, or for that matter, the designer, composer, director or artists who created this work.[85] They are telling a story, and they use an unconventional style to do so. We interpret that story based on our own experiences and breadth of knowledge which is obviously different from those of the creators, and because of that our conclusions may not be those which were intended. It would be easier if the story were told through action and dialogue like a typical anime, and this story is so novel that it would still be a very engrossing one even without the unconventional style. However, we are given something with that style which other works do not offer. We are given the pleasure of discovering, upon re-watching and researching, hidden meanings and ideas. I say pleasure, because that is what it has been for me, and I assume that because you are reading this book, you are fascinated by this unconventional style of storytelling too.

---

85. Blue, 28.

Where possible I have consulted the voice actresses to get their take on the emotional states and internal struggles of their characters. This is because many of the voice actresses' performances demonstrated a detailed understanding of the character's motivations. Of her performance as Kyubey, Cassandra Morris said, "Kyubey is the most controversial character in anime, and I am honored to bring him to life. I have never played a character that has garnered such a wide range of reactions from people. I've met people who are terrified of him and hate him, others who are torn on whether he's good or evil, and still others who can't get past his furry, adorable exterior. There is no you-either-love-him-or-hate-him with Kyubey, he triggers a wide range of emotions from people... which is, of course, a fantastic feat for a being that doesn't even have emotions."[86] Cristina Vee's portrayal of Homura benefitted from knowing the full story from the beginning, and she added elements of her own interpretation. When I imagine myself in Homura's place, having had to watch Madoka die nearly a hundred times, often in Homura's own arms, the only way to describe how that would make me feel would be "emotionally numb." I was struck by Cristina's stoic portrayal of Homura, and when I asked her if that was what she was trying to communicate when voicing Homura, she became elated that I had picked up on that.[87]

Likewise, when speaking with Sarah Williams about her portrayal of Sayaka, it was clear by both her enthusiasm for the conversation and the questions she asked me in return, that she had done her homework. She had clearly done her own research, and had come across some of the same theories that I had. It was easy to see that she was deeply invested in her character. By incorporating the opinions of the actresses who played the characters, I may not know for certain if I have correctly interpreted the character's motivation, but I can at least back up my own interpretation with the intent of the one who lent her voice and emotions to the character.

---

86. Cassandra Morris, email interview.

87. Personal conversation with Cristina Vee, Space Coast Comic Con, 12 September 2015.

I truly wish I had been given the opportunity to speak with Chiwa Saito, Aoi Yuki, Eri Kitamura, Ai Nonaka, or Kaori Mizuhashi. The holy grail in this quest would have been an interview with Gen Urobuchi, Akiyuki Shinbo, or Gekidan Inu Curry. These are the keepers of the definitive answers about character motivations and symbolic meanings. However, that was simply not in the cards.

I probably missed the mark on some of these interpretations, and other critics will have come to different conclusions than I. On some of it, we may never know the truth, and that is fine. The best part of this whole experience has been the search for answers. This is one of a short list of anime I have watched which improved me as a person. It inspired me to read, or re-read classics of literature and legend. It inspired me to research concepts which I wouldn't have had reason to dive into otherwise. It has been far more than entertainment, and yet it has been ultimately entertaining.

I have written fiction before, but I never put as much into that writing process as this story clearly had put into it. To quote Chuck Sonnenburg, "The plot is meticulously constructed, and for the most part that is a strength."[88] To base each character's story arc on a story from classic literature, and to painstakingly design each scene with meaningful imagery which enhances the story is inspiring as a writer. I hope that the next time I write fiction, I can take lessons learned from *Madoka Magica* to take my own work to the next level.

I have met inspiring people, such as Christine Cabanos, Sarah Williams, Carrie Keranen, Cassandra Lee Morris, and Cristina Vee, who have taken the time to share their thoughts on the characters they voiced. And now that this journey is finally over, I wait, hoping that *Rebellion* is not the last chapter in this saga, although if it was it would be a fine conclusion, because ultimately, despite the show's title, this is Homura's story, and she has finally been given her wish. But hopefully there will be more, and I will dive into that new material with the same enthusiasm that I have done with the content we currently have. I look forward to deciphering

88. Sonnenburg, "An Opinionated Look at: Madoka Magica Episode 1."

that future work, and wrapping that research up neatly as yet another present for the fans.

The intention of this book was to give you knowledge that would enhance your understanding and enjoyment of the *Madoka Magica* universe. Now that you have finished reading, put on some *Madoka Magica*, and watch it all over again. If I have done my job, it should be a whole new experience.

Index

Akemi, Homura 3, 9, 12-16, 18-20, 22, 24, 28, 35-36, 38-40, 42, 43-51, 53-60, 62-67, 69, 70-71, 74, 80-83, 88, 92-93, 96-97, 98, 100-103, 105-106.
Apples 13, 24-25, 50, 61, 63.
Beginnings viii-ix, 14, 16, 22, 61, 65, 98.
Blue, Jed 12-14, 24, 33, 56, 60, 104.
Cabanos, Christine ii, v, 43, 106.
Chrlotte/Bebe 11, 22-23, 57, 62-64, 66, 69, 70, 72, 89.
Cheese 62, 63-64.
Clocks 9, 37, 39, 49, 53, 54, 56-60.
Clover 55-56.
Cutie Honey 85-86.
Diamonds 55, 58-59.
Different Story 41, 91, 100.
Elly 61, 69.
Eternal viii-ix, 10-11, 15, 20-21, 29, 31, 51, 64, 74.
Eyes 22, 31, 47, 59, 60-61, 64, 82, 84.
Faust v, 1-8, 11, 29, 72-73.
Field of Daisies Scene 12, 44, 47-48.
Flower/Daisy 31, 55, 57, 59, 61.
Gears/Cog wheels 54, 58, 62. 67.
Gekidan Inu Curry 6, 53, 68, 69, 106.
Gertrud 25-26, 62, 69
Hamlet 24-27.
Grief Seed 3, 41, 91, 93, 97.
Hero's Journey 23, 41-42, 43.
Homulilly 19, 36-37, 39, 53-54, 58, 67, 72.
Horses 61-62, 68.
Kamijou, Kyosuke 28, 32-35, 76, 78-79, 93, 96.
Kaname, Madoka v, 2, 4, 9, 10-13, 15-16, 18, 18-23, 31, 33, 35-36, 38-42, 43-51, 54-56, 58-60, 64-67, 80-83, 87-88, 91-93, 95-98, 99-103, 105.
Karma 23, 83, 97-98.
Keranen, Carrie ii, 41-42, 51-52, 61, 79-80, 102, 106.
Keys 54-57, 60, 62.
Knight 28-30, 60, 65, 87-88.
Kriemhild Gretchen 4, 6, 39, 58, 64.
Kyubey 2-3, 11-13, 15, 20-23, 28, 32, 40, 43, 44-51, 66-67, 76, 80-81, 83, 88, 90-92, 97-98, 100-102.
Labyrinth 4, 6, 12, 22, 28, 31, 45, 47, 53, 56, 59, 61, 63, 66, 69, 70-71, 80, 101.
Law of Cycles/Law of the Cycle 10, 35, 42, 43-44, 46, 64, 67, 93.
Little Sea-Maid/Mermaid 25, 29-32, 34, 87.
Lord of the Rings 21.
Lotte 36, 39.
Macross/Robotech 21.
Mermaid (as symbol) 25, 28-30, 42, 61, 67.
Miki, Sayaka vi, 3-4, 12, 18-20, 22-25, 28-35, 40-41, 45, 51, 60, 63, 68, 71, 76, 78-80, 83, 84, 87, 92-93, 95-102, 105.
Moon 47, 58-59, 62, 64.
Morris, Cassandra Lee ii, 91, 101, 105-106.
Nagisa Momoe 62, 64.
Nightmare 55-57, 66-67, 71, 84.
Nutcracker 19, 28, 35-40, 48, 58, 65, 67, 73.
Obi Wan Kenobi 21, 41-42.
Oktavia von Seckendorff 12, 25, 28-29, 31, 61, 68.
Ophelia 24-26, 61.
Original Series v, viii-ix, 4, 9, 11, 15, 22, 24, 35, 39, 40, 43-44, 46-51, 53-54, 57-58, 62, 64, 66-68, 72-73, 84, 96, 101, 103.
Paradise Lost 14.
Puella Magi Madoka Magica Portable 26.
Rebellion viii-ix, 7, 12-14, 16, 17-20, 25, 28, 30, 34-40, 43-52, 53-60, 62-69, 70-73, 81, 84, 89, 102-103, 104, 106.
Ribbon 19, 37, 39, 48, 59, 64-66, 87, 104.
Runes 4, 54, 67, 70-74, 89.
Sailor Moon v, 85-87, 90, 93.
Saito, Chiwa viii, 106.
Sakura, Kyoko vi, 12-14, 19-20, 24-26, 28, 30-31, 41, 50-51, 57, 60-61, 63, 66, 67-68, 76-78, 80, 83, 84, 87, 90-93, 95-97, 100.
Salamander 59, 62.
Scissors 62, 69.

Shinbo, Akiyuki   5, 23, 44-46, 51, 53, 65, 69, 106.
Shizuki, Hitomi   19-20, 32-35, 55-57, 66-67, 71, 84, 97, 102.
Sisyphus   35.
Sonnenburg, Chuck   17, 35, 84, 106.
Soul Gem   3, 18-20, 22, 24, 31, 56-62, 66, 95, 97.
Swans   38, 58-59.
Teacup   cover, 51.
Tomoe, Mami   vi, 11-12, 18, 20-24, 26, 29, 35-36, 41-42, 51, 55, 57, 60, 61-62, 64, 70, 78, 79-81, 83, 84, 88, 92-93, 96-103.
Tristan "Arkada" Gallant   52.
Twin Chairs Scene   48-49.
Unicorn   67-68.
Urobuchi, Gen   vi, x, 1, 5-8, 15-16, 21, 23-24, 31, 35-36, 45-46, 51, 54, 83, 106.
Vee, Cristina   ii, 65, 83, 105-106.
Walpurgisnacht   4, 6, 12, 39, 44, 49-50, 83, 96.
Williams, Sarah   ii, 34, 105-106.
Windows   57-59, 66, 68, 104.
Wish   2-4, 10-13, 18, 22-24, 27-29, 32, 35, 38, 42, 44-46, 49-50, 64-65, 76-77, 80-81, 83, 91, 93, 95, 97-100, 101-102, 105-106.
Wraith   15, 74, 93.

References

Akiko, Sugawa. "Children of Sailor Moon: The Evolution of Magical Girls in Japanese Anime," *Nippon.com*, Your Doorway to Japan. Accessed 23 December 2015, www.nippon.com/en/a03904/.

Aoki, Ume. "Design Notes." *Megami*, January 2011. Translation at: *Puella Magi Wiki*. Accessed 23 December 2015, https://wiki.puella-magi.net/Megami_Magazine_2011-01.

Anderson, Hans Christian. *The Little Sea-Maid*. Harvard Classics. Accessed 15 December 2016, http://www.bartleby.com/17/3/4.html.

bcfiscus. "The Origin and Evolution of Magical Girls." *Anime Amino*. Accessed 23 December 2015, http://aminoapps.com/page/anime/1118114/origin-and-evolution-of-magical-girls.

Black, Susa Morgan. "The Swan." *The Order of Bards, Ovates, and Druids*. Accessed 15 December 2015, http://www.druidry.org/library/animals/swan.

Blue, Jed A. *The Very Soil: An Unauthorized Critical Study of Puella Magi Madoka Magica*. Eohippus Press, 2014.

Ejc. "3rd Madoka Magica Film Tops K-ON! Film's Box Office." *Anime News Network*. Accessed 17 October 2015, http://www.animenewsnetwork.com/news/2013-12-22/3rd-madoka-magica-film-tops-k-on-film-box-office.

Gallant, Tristan "Arkada." "Glass Reflection Review of Madoka Magica the Movie: Rebellion." *Youtube*. Accessed 17 October 2015, https://www.youtube.com/watch?v=PujoJKtqHSU.

Gill, Malcolm. "Research Letter 22, SALAMANDERS as SYMBOLS." *Firebreak*. Accessed 15 January 2016, http://www.firebreak.com.au/resletter22.html.

Goethe, Johann Wolfgang von. *Faust Parts I & II*. Translated by A. S. Kline. Poetry in Translation. www.poetryintranslation.com.

Hiramatsu, Masaki. *Puella Magi Madoka Magica: Different Story*. Illustrated by Hanokage. Magica Quartet. Japan: Yen Press, 2014.

Hoffman, E. T. A. *The Nutcracker and the Mouse King*. L R C. Accessed 27 November 2015, www.springhole.net/writing/the_nutcracker_and_the_mouse_king/.

Interview with Akiyuki Shinbo and Gen Urobuchi. *New Type* 2013-09. Accessed 6 December 2015, http://wiki.puella-magi.net/NewType_2013-09.

"Interview with Gen Urobuchi." *Shinjidai no Mixture Magazine BLACK PAST*, June 2011. Translated by user symbv from evageeks forum. Accessed 17 June 2015, https://wiki.puella-magi.net/Shinjidai_no_Mixture_Magazine_BLACK_PAST.

Kuroe, Mura. *Puella Magi Oriko Magica*. Illustrated by Mura Kuroe. Magica Quartet. New York: Yen Press, 2013.

"Magical Girl." *TV Tropes*. Accessed 23 December 2015, http://tvtropes.org/pmwiki/pmwiki.php/Main/MagicalGirl.

Novasylum. "Rebel With A Misguided Cause: How Madoka Magica Rebellion Disregards the Values of Its Own Predecessor." *Reddit*. Accessed 17 December 2015, https://www.reddit.com/r/TrueAnime/comments/1wrc4k/rebel_with_a_misguided_cause_how_madoka_magica/cf4ns48.

Nyaa, Kevin. "The Problems With: Madoka Magica Rebellion." *Youtube*. Accessed 14 May 2015, https://www.youtube.com/watch?v=EEldbOjnn8s.

Puella Magi Madoka Magica the Movie: Rebellion. Directed by Akiyuki Shinbo. Aniplex/Magica Quartet. Japan: 2013.

Puella Magi Madoka Magica the Movie: Eternal. Directed by Akiyuki Shinbo. Aniplex/Magica Quartet. Japan: 2012.

Puella Magi Madoka Magica the Movie: Beginnings. Directed by Akiyuki Shinbo. Aniplex/Magica Quartet. Japan: 2012.

Puella Magi Madoka Magica (TV Series). Directed by Akiyuki Shinbo. Aniplex/Magica Quartet. Japan: 2011.

Puella Magi Madoka Magica Portable. Japan: Bandai Namco Entertainment, 2012.

"Puella Magi Madoka Magica Trivia." *Internet Movie Data Base*. Accessed 29 December 2015, http://www.imdb.com/title/tt1773185/trivia?ref_=tt_trv_trv.

Puella Magi Production Notes. Japan: SHAFT, 2011.

Puella Magi Wiki, accessed 29 December 2015, https://wiki.puella-magi.net. Note: Normally, Wiki sites are considered an unreliable resource because anyone can post their own opinion on the site, and the material can change with the public consensus. However, when the subject of the research is public opinion, such as discussion of themes and impressions of a creative work, a wiki site captures the exact substance of the researcher's focus. Not only that, but so many translations of interviews can be found there, and nowhere else. Finally, the transcripts from panel Q&A sessions are invaluable, since nobody can be at all of the events where such discussions take place, and the wiki site is the only repository of such records.

"The World Factbook." *Central Intelligence Agency*. Accessed 14 May 2015. https://www.cia.gov/library/publications/the-world-factbook/geos/ja.html.

Ransom, Ko. "Nico Character Chat with Kazuo Koike and Gen Urobuchi." *Anime News Network*, 29 Jan 2012. Accessed 10 Jan 2016. www.animenewsnetowrk.com/feature/2012-01-29.

Shakespeare, William. *The Tragedy of Hamlet, Prince of Denmark*. Accessed 10 January, 2016. http://shakespeare.mit.edu/hamlet/full.html

Sonnenburg, Chuck. "An Opinionated Look at: Madoka Magica." *SF Debris*. Accessed 16 June 2015, http://sfdebris.com/videos/anime.php.

Starbird, Margaret. "Unicorns." *Sacred Union in Christianity*. Accessed 17 December 2015, http://www.margaretstarbird.net/unicorn.html.

"Swan Meaning and Symbolism." *What's Your Sign*. Accessed 15 December 2015, http://www.whats-your-sign.com/swan-meaning-and-symbolism.html.

"The Four Sisters of the Fourth Anti-Tank Helicopter Squad are Celebrated One Last Time!" *Tokyo Otaku Mode*. Accessed 21 December 2015, http://otakumode.com/news/51a149bf8ccdf39e1300d1e4/The-Four-Sisters-of-the-Fourth-Anti-Tank-Helicopter-Squad-are-Celebrated-One-Last-Time!.

"Urobuchi Gen Retires After Receiving Internet Criticism." *Anime Maru*, May 7, 2014. Accessed 14 May 2015. http://www.animemaru.com/urobuchi-gen-retires-after-receiving-internet-criticism/

Urobuchi, Gen. Material booklet included with the *Rebellion* limited edition Blu-ray. Accessed 18 December 2015. Translated by anon. https://wiki.puella-magi.net/Rebellion_Material_Book#Message_from_Gen_Urobuchi_.28Screenplay.29.

Volger, Christopher. "The Hero's Journey." *Storytech Literary Consulting*. Accessed 17 December 2015, http://www.thewritersjourney.com/.

"What is Dark Fiction?" *Wise Geek*. Accessed 16 June 2015, http://www.wisegeek.com/what-is-dark-fiction.htm.

About the Author

Brian McAfee has been active in the anime community for a very long time. He first got into collecting anime in the late 1980s and has been running clubs, attending as many cons as his budget will allow ever since. He even tried his hand at running a con recently. He was the fan art and fiction moderator on Robotech.com for seven years and is active on Anime-Planet. com, where he posts reviews and recommendations for anime when he has the time. He has made many friends in the American anime industry. For the last two decades he has been on active duty with the U. S. Air Force and looks forward to transitioning to his next, more anime-centric career.

Brian is a graduate student at American Military University pursuing a Masters degree in Ancient and Classical History. He is married with a single teenage daughter who is (to his great delight) also hopelessly addicted to anime.

Made in the USA
San Bernardino, CA
29 May 2020